Snow on the Ben

A guide to the 'Real' Inverness & Highlands

First published in Great Britain
By Kessock Books 2014

Copyright (c) 2014 by Rab MacWilliam

A CIP catalogue record for this book is available from
the British Library

ISBN 978-0-9930296-0-8

Printed by FTRR Printers,
60 Grant Street,
Inverness, IV3 8BS

Preface

'Remembrance of things past is not necessarily the remembrance of things as they were'

I wish I'd said that, but Marcel Proust got there before me. This observation by the French aesthete is probably as close as anyone can get to describing the book you are currently holding in your hands.

I was born and bred in Inverness, then a smaller, less busy place than the city it has become today, and I enjoyed a happy, carefree childhood in the town. However, as I grew older I became increasingly aware that another, more exciting world existed in the lands beyond Daviot, and I spent my teenage years trying mentally to obliterate the fact that I lived in a wee Highland town and to convince myself that I was, in reality, a folk-blues guitarist who resided in Greenwich Village. Eventually, I couldn't wait to leave the place. Therefore, it's something of an irony that today, forty years later in my adopted home city of London, I am spending my dotage trying to remember those years I once tried so hard to forget.

I was born in 1951, the first child of a Merkinch father and a Caithness mother, lived in the Crown area, and attended the Crown School and Royal Academy until I left for Edinburgh University in 1969. I flitted back and fore for a few years until I finally settled in 1974 in London, and I've lived here ever since. My visits back home became less frequent, as many of my friends and family gradually dispersed and because I became a Londoner, with my memories of Inverness fading away as my attachment to the town became more tenuous and, I felt, increasingly irrelevant as I settled into my new life in the city.

However, a couple of factors recently began to alter my perspective on Inverness. First, the debate over Scottish independence reignited my interest in the history of my homeland, particularly the Highlands. Then a conversation with my sister Margaret, also a resident of London, about some of our grannie's words and phrases, led me to reflect on how important the town really was to me, and to realise the intriguing, perverse and, in some ways, unique, nature of the wee place. I began to recall, with affection and nostalgia, the people, the places, the idiomatic and unforgettable use of language, the mischievous wit, the abhorrence of pretension, the often hilarious mishaps, foibles and scandals, and much else: this was the town which made me the person I am today. And I slowly, and unexpectedly, rediscovered a pride in, and a further unexpected affection for, my Inverness roots. *Snow on the Ben* is the result of these reflections.

Last summer I began writing the book as something of a joke, a daft idea to pass an hour or two. I was on holiday in the north of Majorca, and it was hot. Being a peely-wally, I decided to escape the sun and found myself compiling an etymological guide, in a spoof academic style, to the Inverness tongue. I emailed a few entries to a couple of old schoolmates, and their enthusiasm encouraged me to continue. Over the following months, the idea evolved to embrace other aspects of Inverness as we remembered it. Interest in the book slowly spread and a few more old friends from the town became members of what I grandiosely, and self-mockingly, termed the 'colloquium'.

Without the help and support of my Inverness contemporaries and others the book could not conceivably have reached this stage. The more I wrote, the more the years peeled away, prompted by the comments, memories, anecdotes and suggestions which my friends supplied. In the Introduction I describe, as best I can, our intentions in compiling the book, and I feel we have largely succeeded in what we attempted to do. We leave you, the reader, to judge, and we hope you can send us your views on this claim, as well as any topics you feel we could or should have covered. Please contact us on info@kessockbooks.com with your suggestions and comments.

I have been a book and magazine publisher, editor and writer for more years than I care to remember, but I do not recall ever in my career having being involved with such warm-hearted, insightful and admirable people, nor have I enjoyed writing anything which has afforded me as much fun and pleasure as *Snow on the Ben*. For me, it has been a nostalgic journey, which has reminded me that one's oldest mates are and will always be one's closest mates. I thank you all, dear friends, for everything.

Acknowledgements

There are several people I'd like to thank for their contributions and support during the preparation of this book, in particular Anne Beech, Mike and Minnie Clark, Hilary Lawson, Anne MacLeod, George and Margaret MacWilliam, Brian Urquhart and John Watt. Also thanks to Mike Clark for his 'Invernessian's View of the World' illustration on page 18 and to Merrill MacWilliam for providing a detail of her splendid drawing of Ben Wyvis on page 17. Merrill is a gifted local illustrator and artist, and her work can be appreciated and ordered from www.merrillmacwilliam.com.

Richard, Kevin and the people at ForThe Right Reasons have enthusiastically embraced the project and have been very helpful in designing, printing and promoting the book.

Finally, I could not have written this book without the (unwitting) assistance of the many Invernessians I have known, and whose company I have much enjoyed, over the years. I hope that you all enjoy reading the entries which follow and that snow will continue to fall on the Ben.

Rab MacWilliam, London, September 2014

Introduction

'Yer seein' it, mun...'

Snow on the Ben is a book on Inverness, but not necessarily an Inverness you will recognise from reading other brochures and publicity booklets on the town.

Informative and well produced though these guides and books are, they generally focus on stirring historical events and on people and places of interest to the visitor, and pay scant attention to the less documented popular culture and history of the town and its many thousands of inhabitants. In this book, we certainly have no wish to dismiss or belittle these other publications. Rather, you should regard *Snow on the Ben* as a complementary or companion volume: an antidote of sorts to the prevailing wisdom as presented by the more conventional promotional material.

The existing guides serve an admirable purpose in presenting to the visitor a sense of the popularly accepted history and the undoubted natural beauty of the Inverness area, and much of what they say is interesting and valuable. However, they normally tend to a 'land o' the shinin' heather', romanticised and sanitised version of a town and culture which, in truth, never really existed, at least in the sense in which it is today so appealingly presented: a cosy Brigadoon with beguilingly coquettish lassies and brawny, kilted laddies skipping the Highland fling at street corners; fiercely contested caber-tossing competitions on the High Street; tartan-tammied shepherds urging their flocks up the heather-lined braes; wizened locals dispensing Gaelic lore and ancient Celtic wisdom to enthralled passers-by; thatched ale-houses, wisps of peat smoke drifting lazily from their crooked wee chimneys, offering drams of single malt whisky, shortbread and haggis; a profusion of shrines to the saintly Bonnie Prince Charlie and his heroic Jacobite brethren; the surrounding mountains and glens providing a sanctuary for proud stags and noble clan chiefs; while permeating this rugged yet charming dreamscape is a 'quality of life', a pervasive sense of spiritual harmony rarely found elsewhere. Although this idyllic vision is, admittedly, a somewhat exaggerated encapsulation of most guidebooks' descriptions of the town, it does, to a greater or lesser degree, approximate to the image they so vigorously propagate.

Snow on the Ben, however, reveals the reality behind this enchanting perspective on bucolic Highland life, and shows that the town's dominant 'clan and tartan' image, although retaining a number of wistful proponents, is largely a Victorian invention: a misleading representation of the town as a Gaelic Garden of Earthly Delights. This idealised fiction, however, is quite understandable. Inverness is, from a business point of view, little different to other British resorts: all tourist areas seek to optimise their assets, real or imaginary. We all have to make a living and, this being the case, why permit fact to sully legend, as it is legend which helps to oil the commercial wheels of this Royal Burgh?

Despite what may appear, at first glance, to be a less than misty-eyed description of the town, *Snow on the Ben* has not been written in order to denigrate or disparage Inverness: indeed, quite the opposite. The book has been produced by a small group of old friends who were born and brought up in the town between the 1950s and 1970s, and most of them continue to live here. One is naturally proud of one's origins, and this book's contributors are no exception to such a sentiment. The pages which follow are suffused with a deep and enduring fondness for Inverness:

its people, culture, language and history, and a nostalgic and almost indefinable affection for the old place, with its fascinating and turbulent history dating back to early medieval times.

As with most tourist areas, there is another side to Inverness. It has always been a working town (or, rather, city as it is today), with its own eccentricities, foibles, idiosyncrasies and, in particular, its diverse and, to the untrained ear, frequently incomprehensible lexicon of words, phrases and dialects. This is only to be expected from a settlement which has over the centuries attracted Picts, Gaels, Ancient Scots, Scandinavians, French, Flemish, Dutch, Anglo-Saxons, East European and English visitors and invaders, to list just a few of the peoples who have made their way through this confluence of military and trading routes, its geographical location in the centre of the Highlands being an important factor in its role as a cultural crossroads. So Inverness's linguistic complexity is understandable: over the centuries there has evolved a native dialect, much of which is unique to the area.

Snow on the Ben is an attempt by a group of people who grew up 'speaking Inverness' to explain to the uninformed, who may be perplexed by what they are hearing, the history, etymology and meaning of these words and phrases. In so doing, we have found it necessary on occasion to veer away from the purely linguistic and to reflect on the history, people and places that have created and defined this splendid old Burgh.

Most of the selected words and phrases relate to the town. However, a few originate from the area bordered to the south by Daviot (from the Pictish 'Deimidh, meaning 'a strong place' and used in this book as a fanciful synonym for the beginning of the Lowlands); to the north by the Black Isle (actually a peninsula, the Gaelic term being 'an t-Eilan Dubh'); to the west by Beauly, the gateway to the Western Isles; and to the east by Nairn, beyond which lie the 'Doric' lands of north-eastern Scotland. The word 'Doric' was originally applied by the ancient Greek Athenians to the Dorians of Sparta, whom they regarded as uncouth and untrustworthy peasants.

The entries in *Snow on the Ben* are organised alphabetically but not in a pedantic, tedious fashion. We have, where appropriate, adopted a mischievous, irreverent style, while also attempting to ensure strict factual accuracy. We sincerely hope no one will interpret our efforts as either patronising or offensive. This has never been our intention. The information, anecdotes and comments herein are offered in a spirit of good humour, in keeping with the typical Inverness blend of mock surliness, sharp insight, wickedly sardonic wit, warm heartedness and absence of pomposity. It is as authoritative a guide as we can manage to Inverness's intriguing demotic meanderings.

'It's worse yer improveen...'

Inverness was first inhabited during the late Neolithic period, around the 4th millennium BC, some while after the Ice Age had made its excuses and headed north. However, one can understand why a discerning listener might think that some of these early settlers have not yet got round to leaving the place. For example, try the following:

'How's the crack, ye gurning bodhach?' 'Yer seein' it, mun.' 'Ah hear ye had a bit of a boorach last night.' 'Aye it was wi'a scaffie ootside the Fluke. He was a blethering old bachle of a coast-wester and I was blootered, so I skelped him.' 'Och, it's worse yer improveen. It's a grand day, tho.' 'Aye, but there's snow on the Ben.'

See what I mean? It's clearly on nodding terms with what we understand as today's English, but much of the conversation sounds like it's being conducted between two grunting, hairy, deerskin-draped old boys in a dingy wee cave overlooking the Beauly Firth.

So imagine you're a tourist visiting Inverness, the 'Capital of the Highlands', and sipping a wee 'dram' in a public house in the heart of this bustling, modern city. Two local gentlemen, perhaps in slightly disheveled though respectable attire, have just sat down opposite you, and, judging by their discussion, they are speaking in an apparently alien tongue. What on earth are they talking about? Well, if you read this book, you'll find out. By the time you have finished, you should be able to interpret the above paragraph in the following manner:

'How are you, old chap? You appear somewhat out of sorts, if I may say so.' 'I am in fine spirits, thank you.' 'I gather you encountered a spot of bother yesterday evening.' 'Yes, indeed I did. A verbose local council worker from the Western Isles irritated me outside a local public house and, as I had consumed an unwise quantity of alcoholic beverage, we had something of an altercation.' 'Dear, dear, old fellow, you really must learn to control yourself. However, it is a delightful day today.' 'Yes, it most certainly is. But have you noticed the adverse climatic conditions currently prevailing on the nearby range of mountains: could it perhaps be a portent of winter?'

You may not immediately understand the Inverness version, but there is a certain, no-nonsense brusque poetry to it. Put aside, for the moment, your mother tongue. After reading this book you'll be a true cheuchter, blethering and havering away like the rest of us. If you've never heard 'bodach' or 'whinner', you've come to the right place. And if you like your information enlivened by anecdotes, entertainment and a liberal dose of wry, affectionate humour, you've certainly come to the right book.

Ben Wyvis
By Merrill MacWilliam

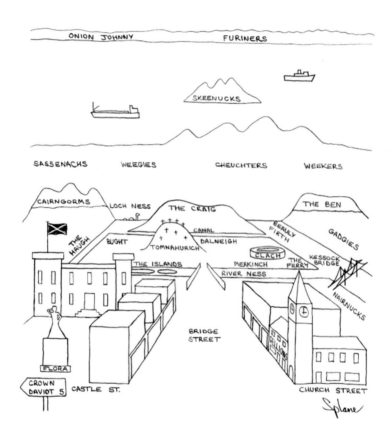

The Invernessian
view of the world
By Mike Clark

Snow on the Ben

A guide to the 'real' Inverness & Highlands

'*Ach*' *(hard 'ch'):* an exclamation, usually preceding a sentence, in common usage in Inverness. Although in its three-letter brevity, it appears synonymous with the equally ubiquitous 'och' (*see below*), its Germanic tones betray an element of censoriousness and a degree of denigration in what is about to follow, while 'och' has a softer, more sympathetic, Gaelic feel. 'Ach' strode tetchily westwards across the Doric lands or northwards over the Grampians and made its grumpy, judgemental home in Inverness. 'Ach', in this context, seems to have nothing in common with the place name prefix 'Ach', which stems from the Gaelic 'achad', meaning 'a field', as in Achiltibuie, Achnasheen and others. The small town of Avoch, in the Black Isle and across the Moray Firth from Inverness, is pronounced 'Och' but comes from yet another etymological root (or route), ie French, as it was originally spelt Auoch and was possibly a Huguenot settlement dating from the 18th century. (Another theory is that, when God was naming the world, the Black Isle was last on his list. He was understandably tired and so, on encountering the wee town, he said 'Och, that'll do'. However, this plausible theory doesn't explain the spelling.)

Bachle *(hard 'ch' as in 'loch')*: an expression of mild contempt tinged with justifiably suspicious distrust. Could have its origins in the Old Scots word 'bauchle' (scruffy, worn out, and usually wearing cheap old shoes). In *Kidnapped*, RL Stevenson uses the verb 'bauchled' to mean 'bungled'. In Inverness, a 'bachle' is normally a male of a certain age, small and stocky in stature, bow-legged, bald (*see 'baldy-heid' below*) and often to be found propped up in a corner of the Gellions Public Bar (*see below*), singing 'The Dark Island' into an empty pint glass.

Baldy-heid: an observation guaranteed to incite ire in the intended target. A 'baldy-heid' is a follicularly challenged individual, normally male but occasionally female, whose head is, apart from perhaps a few stray wisps, hairless, and pale, pink or sunburnt depending on occupation or lack thereof. A condition common among 'meenisters' (*see below*) of the Church of Scotland, school teachers and centre halves. In males, an attempt to disguise this condition with a flat cap can lead to ridicule, particularly on blustery days. Women 'baldy-heids' wear black curly wigs which, when these females are in a 'blootered' (*see below*) state, tend to slide slowly down the forehead and land on the owner's whisky and blackcurrant, a spectacle from which much merriment is derived.

***Beauly** (pronounced Bewlee)*: attractive old village twelve miles to the west of Inverness, and regarded as the eastern boundary for 'coast-westers' (*see below*). This is where one of 'The Road to the Isles' begins. From the French 'beau-lieu': 'beautiful place' (attributed to Mary Queen of Scots). Beauly contains one large central square (originally a cattle market) and several posh little boutique shops, which service the expensive homes in its hinterland, and a 15th-century Priory. Beauly is the heartland of Clan Fraser country, a clan of French origin who arrived in Scotland in the 12th century. Fraser is today one of the most common surnames in the Inverness area. The wee place dominates 'shinty' (*see below*) in the immediate Inverness area. The River Beauly is famous for salmon fishing (and crafty poachers).

Belting: not a pleasant experience. It is a savage battering, which renders the recipient senseless and in a pitiable state. The term probably stems from the days when a belt was used to administer punishment in the local schools. Belting' is more ferocious, with longer lasting effects, than similar acts of wanton violence, such as a 'skelp' (a slap in the face) or a 'kick in the erse' (self-explanatory). A local bar of some social standing, which has now gone but which for sake of convenience we will call the Lochiel, once displayed a sign saying "Please do not ask for credit, as a belt in the mouth can often offend'.

Ben: 'ben' has two meanings, stemming from different etymological origins. The word is most often used locally to refer to a rounded mountain and derives from the Gaelic 'beinn'. In this sense, 'bens' are everywhere, including Ben Fionnlaidh and Ben Wyvis (from which the title of this book is taken: there is also a Little Wyvis, which stands at over 2,500 feet in height, and its parent is significantly higher). The Gaelic word 'carn' also describes a mountain (think Cairngorm) and means a rocky hill. The other meaning of 'ben' has its meaning a room, and in this context means origin in the Old English word 'binnan', 'inner' or 'interior'. You may have encountered the phrase 'but 'n ben', with reference to a holiday cottage or having read 'The Broons' in the *Sunday Post*. This was a small dwelling, wherein lived the local peasantry, the 'but' being the section of the house where the animals slept in the winter, and the 'ben' referring to the rest of the house. A frequently heard phrase in Inverness is 'ben the house' meaning 'in the house' ('hoose' would be the preferred description south of Daviot, but we speak proper English in this fair city). 'Where's thon Tomuck got to the now? Och, he's ben the front room having a wee dram'. This latter usage of the word is probably regarded in the sophisticated Crown area (*see below*) as somewhat vulgar, but it should be said that the Crown area regards most things as somewhat vulgar. 'Thomas has retired to the drawing room to write tasting notes on a glass of twenty-year-old single malt' would be the Crown response as to Tomuck's whereabouts.

Black Bull: today, a riverside hangout for wealthy metro-crofters and ever-hopeful Clachars *(see below)*. In years gone by, it was a bar famed in Merkinch *(see below)* history.

Phrases of relevance include 'Who flung the Black Bull over the Black Bridge? Aye, but who flung him back again?' Also, 'I can get that ('blethers', *see below*) for the price of a half pint in the Black Bull'. Used to be frequented by Lascar sailors from the Harbour, prostitutes from Elgin, a few confused Skeenucks (*see below*), farmers from Wick (*see 'Weekers' below*), travelling people *(see 'tinkers' below)*, a few scowling Glaswegians (*'Weegies'*) and several other intriguing characters. A proud establishment which today bears the name 'The Waterfront', and is obviously marketing itself at even more metro-crofters (how many of these people can there be?).

Blayzeen: a corruption of the Anglo-Saxon 'blazing', which appears to stem from military usage and refers to 'blazing away' with a rifle in an erratic, irresponsible, careless (or deliberately murderous) manner. Hanoverian soldiers were adept at this tactic in the years immediately following the 1745 Jacobite Rebellion, particularly when an innocent Highlander was standing in front of them. Today in Inverness the word describes an unwise over-indulgence in alcohol, a not uncommon occurrence, which confers on the imbiber a misguided sense of inviolability. Generally proclaimed with a degree of emphatic certainty ("Ah'm blayzeen"), which contrasts markedly with the mental state and physical capability of the confider. It is normally the precursor to 'blootered' (*see below*).

***Blethers*:** possibly originating in Edinburgh, a prim Saxon settlement, otherwise known as 'England in kilts', which lies to the south of Daviot. 'Blethers' ranges from crazed ranting via lying to your partner about your sexual prowess to scheming and duplicitous venality. A practitioner of blethers is known as a 'bletherskite' and described as 'talking shite' (self-explanatory). 'Blethering' is the normal means of communication in the Inverness area.

***Blootered*:** an inability to remain coherent and upright due to an unwisely excessive intake of 'drams' (*see below*). The widespread usage of 'blootered' dominates the many other similar euphemisms, such as 'blayzeen' (*see above*), 'gu'ered' ('guttered', with the two 't's absent: the glottal stop is, however, not uncommon in the Gaelic tongue and does not necessarily imply inebriation), 'pished' (self-explanatory) and 'steamin' (originally a Glaswegian term from the days when the bars shut on Sundays and the only place to get a drink was on a steamboat trip down the Clyde). As you may imagine, these words become increasingly slurred as the evenings draw inexorably onward to their inevitable conclusions. ('Blooter' can also mean to wallop a football with an ineptly aimless ferocity but, as our footballers are all delicately skillful ball-players, this is usually a term employed in the Lowlands south of Daviot.)

Bodach (*'ch' as 'bachle'*): a 'mannie' (*see below*), pal or workmate: similar, in its affectionate sense of comradeship, to the London East End 'geezer'. 'Bodachs' can be either 'old' or 'wee', but never female. 'Cailleach' (*see below*) is the mature female equivalent of 'bodach' but is rarely used, as Invernessian women are too sensible to speak in anything but standard English. All males are 'bodachs' of one sort or another, unless they owe you money in which case they are 'whinners' (*see below*). 'Bodach' is also Gaelic for 'penis' but, for a number of reasons, this semantic similarity must be coincidental.

Bogey *(pronounced 'boogie')*: inventive local 'bairns' (young children) constructed these as a means of transport. They made them from old haddock or herring fish boxes, recycled pram wheels and rotting planks of wood. They rarely had brakes or steering, so were perceived by pedestrians as something of a hazard, to be best (and quickly) avoided. Used for getting 'messages' (*see below*) from the shops, bags of coke (no, not what you may be thinking: rather, cinders from the local gasworks) for their grannies' fires, hurtling down braes and other assorted pieces of anti-social mischief.

Boke: the almost inevitable consequence of being 'blootered' (*see above*). To 'boke' is to evacuate, rapidly and with alarming ferocity, the foul-smelling contents of one's stomach, usually onto a policeman's freshly laundered uniform, the floor of a public house or one's partner's lap. Under no circumstances attempt to repair the damage. Feign unconsciousness, and you may get away with it. Evidence of 'boking' is normally visible on pavements on a Sunday morning stroll down Inverness High Street.

Boorach *(again, a hard 'ch')*: an untidy and unsightly jumble, or an unplanned, confusing or inexplicable set of circumstances. Originates from the Gaelic 'burach', meaning 'a mess'. A term often used by aunties and grannies when they have visitors: 'och, the room's a right old boorach' (although they've spent all morning tidying it up), and also by followers of Caley Thistle (*see 'traitors' below*) when discussing their 'defence'. May also be employed ('a bit of a boorach') when males enact hostile virility rituals outside public houses at closing time, a fairly frequent demonstration of stumbling bravado. It's a handy word generally, as it can be used to describe any unusual behaviour which you can't be bothered to explain: 'och, it was jist a boorach'.

Bowsher boy *(pronounced not as the wooden archery weapon, but rather as 'ow' in 'down')*: once a familiar sight on the streets of Inverness. A young lad, usually in his early teens, who wobbled around on his old bike with a steel-framed basket attached to its handlebars. This receptacle contained precariously perched cuts of beef, lamb, chicken etc. These were parceled up by a butcher and were delivered to local homes by the 'bowsher boy'. The word is almost certainly an Inverness corruption of the French 'bouchon', meaning 'butcher'. A common rite of passage when one became a 'bowsher boy' was for the butcher's staff to lock the new employee for an hour or so in the floor-to-ceiling deep freeze, which was crammed with unpleasant bits of dead 'coos'. If I sound bitter, it's because that's what they did to me (and probably to my father who was also a 'bowsher boy'). May those sadists burn in the seventh circle of Hell alongside Atilla the Hun and his villainous acolytes.

Brae (*as in donkey noise*): a term also used south of Daviot but common in the town. The name describes a hill, often beside a river. Derives from Old Norse for 'an eyelash', a somewhat tenuous connection. Stephens Brae doglegs from the old Royal Academy (*see below*) to the High Street and was used for sledging by a few foolhardy and now consequently less mobile residents. The Raining's Stairs, which connects the Crown with Castle Street and is named after Raining's School, is a brae but unusually it is stepped, narrow and very steep. Raining's School, incidentally, was originally built by the Society for the Propagation of Christian

29

Knowledge (compared to whom, the Wee Frees (*see below*) could be regarded as fun-loving, jovial pranksters) and which in the 1960s became The Doc's Club, a haven of youthful high jinks and harmless pagan skullduggery: a neat irony, indeed.

Brahan Seer: a visionary and prophet who may or may not have existed, but probably did. A 'coast-wester' (*see below*), his name was Coinneach Odhar, anglicised into Kenneth MacKenzie, who lived in Brahan Castle, Dingwall, the home of the Earls of Seaforth, in the 17th century. He predicted the Caledonian Canal ('one day ships will sail round the back of Tomnahurich') and warned that when five bridges were built over the River Ness, then mayhem would follow. The fifth bridge was built over the River Ness in August 1939. The following month Hitler invaded Poland. Seemingly, the footbridges were not counted, thereby diminishing the potency of the prediction. There were several other predictions of that ilk, or so we are informed.

'Brochan lom': or, in full, 'brochan lom, tana lom, brochan lom na sughain', to the tune of 'a doo fell aff, a doo fell aff, a doo fell aff a dyke' (if you don't know this, I'm afraid I can't help you). This is a cheery, tuneful ditty, which was often heard in Inverness, normally from grannies or aunties who had perhaps a couple of glasses of sherry ('och, jist one, then') more than they should have done. It is an example of 'Gaelic mouth music', the enchanting singing of 'coast-wester' (*see below*) weaver women at their looms. It is the first verse of a nonsense song, and translates as 'porridge thin and meager / porridge made from sowan' ('sowan' being an oatcake or scone). 'Brochan lom' is also heard as a drinking song in the film version of Compton MacKenzie's book *Whisky Galore!* and it has been recorded by, among others, Calum Kennedy (*see below*) and Robin Hall and Jimmie McGregor, a singing duo often featured in 1960s TV shows. Also, 'Briochan' was the Druid foster-father of the Pictish King Brude (*see 'Craig Dunain' below*), but he does not seem to have been related to porridge in any way (although he probably ate it).

Bught Park (*'gh' as in resonant throat-clearing exercise prior to expectoration*): a large expanse of uninviting, pot-holed public scrubland to the south of the town close to the western road to Loch Ness. 'Bught' is Gaelic for 'sheep pen'. Contains numerous 'football pitches', an Ice Rink (the construction of which necessitated the destruction of Bught House, an 18th-century Georgian dwelling), caravan park, sports stadium, and is home to regular funfairs (*see 'Shows' below*). Also home to an Aquadome, Leisure Centre and Registrar office, which contains a centre for local genealogy and which is the archive depository for the Highland region. So today it's not quite the scraggy old 'sheep pen' it used to be. Bounded by the River Ness, Caledonian Canal and Tomnahurich (*see below*).

'Cailin mo ruin-sa...' (*pronounced 'calla ma roonsa'*): it's pretty much a safe bet that, if you ask someone who was born and raised in Inverness, they'll know this as the opening few words of the Gaelic song 'Dearest, my own one, oh won't you be mine'. It's usually the first song wee bairns hear, when they're slyly looking for where Auntie Morag has hidden the sweeties. It's not a bad tune, and I've heard worse lyrics, but it was damned forever when it was interminably and cloyingly warbled by all the smugly smirking, swirling-kilted, cod-Hielan' singers of the 1960s and 1970s, including but certainly not limited to Calum Kennedy (*see below*), The

Alexander Brothers, Andy Stewart, Kenneth McKellar... and everybody's grannies. I heard it so often when I was just a wee thing that I hated it with a vengeance. It's like being locked in a room for a week with John Lennon's appalling 'Imagine' as your only companion. Nevertheless, Gaelic is a fine language for singing: its yearning softness, tenderness and evocative modal phrasing more than compensates for its incomprehensibility to English ears. At impromptu Gaelic 'mouth music' ('puirt-a-beul') events, voices take the place of instruments, and these evenings usually lead to dancing, the 'uisque beatha' ('water of life': whisky) and, inevitably, furtive couplings behind the whins (*see 'whinners' below*). There is a seductive mystical quality to Gaelic music, unless it's 'Cailin mo...' (*See 'Brochan lom' above.*)

***Cailleach*:** a female 'bodach' (*see above*). Not a word in common usage, perhaps because of its slightly pejorative, patronising implications. Inverness men are unwilling to risk incurring the wrath of local women, and rightly so. It's possibly the Hielan' equivalent of the Glaswegian 'hen', although 'cailleach' is a more refined endearment. However, do

33

not use this word unless on intimate terms with addressee, or an indignant 'skelp in the lug' may be the unseemly outcome.

Caledonian Canal: an engineering triumph of a waterway, built by Thomas Telford in the early 19th century, which wends its way from the Beauly Firth down to Fort William, via the three lochs of the Great Glen. Although it must be said that, from Inverness to Dochfour, the countryside is rather flat and dull, as soon as one nears the loch one is struck by the serenity of the surrounding mountains as they sweep down to meet the loch's still, deep waters, and the view down the Great Glen is breathtaking. Only a few miles from the bustling, modern city of Inverness, and one is suddenly in the heart of some of the most majestic, imposing scenery to be found anywhere in the world. It can be a humbling experience, but also a joyous one. Regular cruises operate from Inverness to the loch and back. You should make the effort to take one. (I here declare an interest: my late father set up the first such company, Jacobite Cruises, in the early 1970s, which today continues to operate up and down the canal.) As a kid I used to ride horses, OK, ponies along the towpath. Again, you should have a go, but don't fall in the water. You never know what's in there. (*See 'Loch Ness' below*).

'Camera how? *(articulated in a soft, 'coast-wester' (see below) accent):* this does not refer to the location of the nearest photographic shop. Rather, it is the English language attempt at the Gaelic greeting 'Ciamar tha thu', meaning 'Hello' or 'How are you?' If you're in good spirits, you should reply 'Hagoo ma', which does not imply, as it may sound, that you are insulting your enquirer's mother. It is the English version of 'Tha gu mhath': 'I am well'. Likewise, 'Ochee va' (*hard 'ch'*) is a loose transliteration of the Gaelic 'Oidche mhath', meaning 'good night'. These phrases remain in use, although more often heard from grannies and aunties than from pink-haired youth with rings in their noses. Interestingly, there is not a word for either 'Yes' or 'No' in Gaelic. So if you ask 'Did you go out last night?' in Gaelic, the response is either 'I did go out' or 'I didn't go out' (or 'Mind your own business'). Such a response is more precise than the English language, and removes any possible ambiguity. And let's not get started on 'Ceud mile failte'… oh, all right: it means 'A hundred thousand welcomes' and has been written on all Inverness Burgh boundary signs since time immemorial, or at least since I can remember.

Castle, Inverness: *(Before you begin reading this entry, you should be aware that the following description is my - the author's - personal opinion, and does not necessarily reflect the views of any other contributor to this volume, a few of whom feel that I am being less than generous to this monstrosity.)* When gazing idly around the Inverness townscape, you may observe (in fact, it's impossible to miss) a red sandstone building perched on a hill overlooking the Ness Bridge (*see below*) and offering a panoramic view of the town. This architectural excrescence is known as Inverness 'Castle', described by Bill Bryson, with his tongue clearly buried deep in his cheek if not halfway down his throat, as 'adorably over the top'. To me, it's a continuing mystery why this castellated calamity, which is so hideously ugly that its plans would have been rejected by Stalin and the architect immediately executed, was allowed to be erected in the middle of such stunning natural grandeur as that which surrounds Inverness: but that's what they did in 1836. Shoving a brass statue of St Flora MacDonald ('Speed bonny boat, like a bird on the wing…') in front of it fifty years later only added to its appallingly kitsch appearance. However, before this Ruritanian 'fortified' shambles was dumped on the hill, there had been several intriguing castles on the site over the centuries, beginning with an earth and timber fortress established by King David I in the 12th century. It was occupied by English troops during the early-14th century Wars of Independence, but shortly afterwards it was destroyed by Robert the Bruce. Its ownership then passed between the clans Donald and MacKintosh, until the Earl of Mar in the 15th century built a stone castle, which was enlarged by the next tenant, the Earl of Huntly, although this was besieged and captured by Queen Mary in 1562. (During the siege, she lived in Queen Mary's House in Bridge Street, which was the oldest existing building in Inverness until 1968 when, in an act of wanton lunacy, it was demolished to make way, eventually, for the Highlands and Islands Development Board HQ.) The castle was then captured and recaptured during the Civil War, and it was re-occupied after the 1715 Jacobite Rebellion by General Wade (Hanoverian road-builder-in-chief: 'If you'd seen these roads before they were made / You'd have lifted your hands and blessed General Wade', although the new roads were used mainly by Prince Charlie and his troops on their way south in 1745). In 1746 Charlie and his retreating Jacobites blew up the castle, and today there are more than a few locals who feel that such an act should be replicated. This absurd example of early-Victorian 'Highlandism', however, does have a few points in its favour, in particular the splendid view southwards down the river to the Great Glen. Also, its shaded surrounds have been used over the years as a cover for lovers' trysts and teenage wine tasting, and it's only a short amble from the Gellions (*see below*). There is continuing talk about converting the building into an art gallery, museum or tourist centre, rather than using it in its current capacity as a courthouse and prison for local rogues, vagabonds and 'sheep shaggers' (*see 'ovine outrage' below*). However, the clincher: as tourists and visitors appear to enjoy strolling round its grounds and, as no one ever went broke underestimating public taste, let's all celebrate this magnificent addition to the skyline of our ancient Royal Burgh. (*This final sentence should shut them up: author.*)

Cheuchter (*first 'ch' as in 'chips, second as 'loch'*): the vulgar spelling of the Gaelic 'teuchter'. A word used, normally in a condescending sense, to describe someone who originates from further north and/or west in Scotland than you do. In Inverness, a cheuchter is normally an inhabitant of the Western Isles (*see 'coast-wester' below*). Being called a cheuchter implies a certain lack of sophistication, a degree of unworldliness and a fondness for 'drams' (*see below*). This stereotype is, of course, totally erroneous, I've been told to say (by cheuchters). However, it's true to say that, in my experience, cheuchters are some of the friendliest, most intelligent and best-educated people I have had the pleasure of meeting (this is a personal opinion, and unprompted). (*See 'Sassenach' below.*)

Citadel: one of the oldest parts of the town, located across the river from the Merkinch (*see below*) and next to Inverness Harbour. Named after the substantial, pentagonal structure erected in 1655 during the Cromwellian Protectorate. Was capable of holding a garrison of 1,000 men, whose function was to subdue the Highlands (these people do persist…). Only lasted until the 1660 Restoration, and the building was dismantled two years later to provide stone for a bridge over the river. Only the clock tower remains, on Cromwell Road, although recently doubts have been expressed about its provenance. The first quay on the Harbour was built in 1675 on Shore Street, and a second, the Thornbush Quay, followed in 1815 across the river in an area where shipbuilding (*see below*) began in the 11th century. A third quay was built in 1977. The Citadel bar, now closed, was also located on Shore Street, catering for the thirsty sailors and Harbour workers, and a rough old bar it was, staging, as it did, many splendid 'boorachs' (*see above*). Also, the Citadel was home to the first Inverness football club: Citadel FC. The club was one of the original members of the Highland League in 1893, won the League title only once (1909) and withdrew from the competition in 1935, folding just before WWII. The Citadel was once one of Inverness's most intriguing old areas, but it has now been largely converted into, yes, 'executive' flats.

Clachnacuddin FC *('ch' as in 'loch')*: the last remaining Highland League football club in Inverness, after Caley and Thistle conspired to join forces (*see 'traitors' below*) and greedily grasped the Scottish League shilling. 'Clachnacuddin' is Gaelic for 'stone of the tubs', a rock against which washerwomen used to dry clothing. This symbol of old Inverness currently sits in majestic splendour outside the Town Hall. The club's name – Inverness Clachnacuddin – is universally shortened to 'Clach'. Clach have had a chequered history but are now back in contention. They are known as the 'Lilywhites' (after their white shirts), and play at Grant Street Park in the Merkinch (*see below*). Grant Street was also home to the famous Clach bars, the Argyle and Lochiel, which were always packed before home games until the Clach Club came into being. Clach supporters touch the 'Lucky Stone' on Lochalsh Road for good luck before games (not that it often works).

Clachar (*usual 'ch' pronounciation*): an inhabitant of the old part of Inverness, the Merkinch (*see below*), the area surrounding the home ground of Clachnacuddin FC close to the Ferry (*see below*). Clachars have little in common with the gentry of the Crown area (*see below*) and are, on occasion, patronisingly and unfairly dismissed as idle illiterates. Nothing could be further from the truth: Clachars personify the genuine spirit of old Inverness, unlike some of the arrivistes who malign them.

***Clarty*:** used south of Daviot but also a common Inverness word. Means 'dirty' or 'muddy'. Most frequently used by parents when their wee darlings spill food on their clothes or dirty their knees playing football or skipping or whatever kids do these days. Not nasty or unpleasant, just 'messy'. 'Och, away and wash yersel, ye wee clart'. 'Clarted' is also frequently used as an adjective instead of 'clarty'.

***Clearances*:** the forced removal of Highland crofters and their families from their homes from the mid-18th through the 19th centuries by aristocratic, often absentee landowners and wealthy clan chiefs who rarely visited their territories, aided by the British state, who enclosed their lands into pastures for profitable sheep rearing. Highlanders had been for many years intrepid voyagers, mainly to the Baltic countries, but the period of the Clearances was generally involuntary and markedly greater in scale. This 'emigration' was given added impetus by the government's savage military 'cleansing' of the Highlands in the years following the 1745 Jacobite Rebellion (*see 'Culloden' below*). The 'Year of the Sheep', 1792, was a low point, when thousands of crofters were sent to the North American colonies. Many others were sent to the coast to become fishermen or kelp gatherers, vocations for which they were entirely unsuited, or they were relocated to less fertile areas to scratch out a living. The Clearances were renewed in the early 19th century, with the Duke of Sutherland a particularly cruel and notorious exponent. He taxed his subjects in order to build a 30-metre-high statue of himself on top of Ben Bhraggie overlooking Golspie, a hubristic memorial visible for miles. This statue, known locally as 'The Mannie', has been the regular target of attempted, and so far failed, dislodgements. And Sutherland was only one of the many landlords and aristocrats who profited from the misery of others during the Clearances. This brutal destruction of an ancient way of life and displacement of an entire population continued until well after the Potato Famine of the 1840s, and effectively ended the feudal clan system. The Clearances are still recalled with bitter resentment in the Highlands, as poignantly expressed in this 18th-century poem: 'I see the departure of the heroes / Over the ocean in white-sailed ships / I see the Gael in travail / Rising from their doors / I see the people leaving / For there is no love for them in the North'.

Clootie Well: this lies in Culloden Forest and is today known as St Mary's Well, although it dates from pre-Christian times. A 'cloot' (or 'clout') is a cloth or a rag, and the Celtic inhabitants of the area would soak a brightly coloured cloth in the Well. They would then hang the 'cloot' from the branches of a nearby tree as a votive offering to the local spirits, in order to cure ailments. The Well was visited most often on the Celtic festival of Beltane (1 May) in an attempt to ward off evil spirits for the rest of the year. It's a peaceful spot, if slightly eerie. Munlochy, across the Firth in the Black Isle, is also home to a much visited 'clootie well'.

Coast-wester: a 'cheuchter' (*see above*) from the Western Isles, normally Stornaway. Males are usually called Donald (Donnie), but sometimes Alexander (Alec) or Malcolm (Calum). The standard female name is Morag, but they are often called 'ina', preceded by a male name. I have yet to meet a Torquilina but one must exist. A friend of mine once knew a girl called Iainina, so there is hope. Recognisable by the soft lilting accents. Common phrase is 'Och weel, I shouldn't really, but...' Good at shinty (*see below*), a terrifying pastime involving sticks, huge crofters and broken legs. This bone-shattering sporting propensity aside, however, most 'coast-westers' whom I have known are warm-hearted and friendly people, and usually up for the 'crack' (*see below*).

Colonel Bogey: a tune immortalised in the wartime movie 'The Bridge Over The River Ness' (often referred to erroneously as 'The River Kwai'). 'Hitler has only got one ball...' The tune was written by a band master at Fort George (a brooding Hanoverian hulk a few miles east of Inverness and the only such fort never to have fired a cannonball in anger). He used to row his colonel over to Fortrose Golf Club (across the Beauly Firth) for a few hours of hacking and hooking, and he composed it during one of these frequent trips. 'And poor old Goebbels...'

Courier, Inverness: an institution, the town's local newspaper for almost two hundred years. First published in 1817, it soon became the fiefdom of the Barron family, with Evan Barron assuming the editorship from WW1 until the late 1960s, when Evelyn of That Ilk took over. A broadsheet with an imposing old German Gothic typeface as its masthead, it is still published bi-weekly (Tuesdays and Fridays), and maintained its tradition of retaining the front page for advertising until the Barron family sold it some years ago. Pride of place, I recall, was always reserved for an ad for Balnafettack tatties, with Mario's shop on Eastgate a close second. In 1933, the *Courier* invented the Loch Ness Monster, when it printed the first ever sighting of the beastie under the headline 'Strange Spectacle on Loch Ness', thereby doing more for the local economy than anything before or since. When Bridge Street was being redeveloped in the 1960s, the Barron family refused to move from their old, rickety building, so an office block, Bridge House, now private apartments, was built around the *Courier* office. On the opposite side of Bridge Street, incidentally, is a concrete construction of staggering ugliness, considered by many to be the worst architectural atrocity in the UK. The old *Courier* building still exists, but is occupied by an estate agent, while the newspaper now meets its deadlines from an office beside the Kessock Bridge. Competition comes and goes, but the *Courier* remains, steadfast and worthy.

Crack: not to be confused with the instantly addictive, cocaine-derived narcotic (one of our contributors – all right, me – was once threatened with ejection from an English rehab holiday camp for using the everyday Inverness phrase 'good crack'). Derives from the Gaelic 'craic', meaning 'a good time' or 'a pleasant conversation'. Common usages include 'How's the crack?' to which the normal response is 'yer seein' it, mun' (*see below*). The apparently oxymoronic 'poor crack' refers to an unhappy experience or to the quality of the entertainment being below the required standard.

Craig Dunain: from the Gaelic 'rock of the bird', a hill outside the town boundary on the Fort Augustus/Loch Ness road. Faces Torvean (from the Gaelic 'Tor Bhean', from where St Bean preached to the Picts), another hill overlooking Inverness. Craig Dunain was home to the grandiosely titled Northern Counties District Lunatic Asylum (obviously pre-PC days), the oldest Victorian psychiatric hospital in Scotland, built in 1864. Closed in 2000 and now derelict, although scheduled for re-development. 'Going up the Craig' meant visiting an unfortunately afflicted relative. The nearby Craig Phadrig ('Patrick's rock') is another wooded hill, on top of which sits the remains of a 4th-century BC vitrified fort. Also reputed to have been the residence of King Brude, King of the Picts, in the 6th century AD. A grand view over the Beauly Firth.

Crit: affectionate diminutive for the now long-gone Criterion public house on the corner of Church Street and Baron Taylor's Street (once known as the Black Vennel: a French term for a passageway) which formed part of the historic pub trail beginning at the Fluke, passing through the Gellions (*see below*), dropping in at the Argyle and collapsing at the Clachnaharry Inn. Appropriately, the Gaelic name for Clachnaharry, which marks the western boundary of the town, is 'clach na-aithrigh' meaning 'stone of repentance'. Only brave men undertook this journey, and some still describe the trip in reverential tones, at least those who can remember the adventure.

Crown: a part of town best avoided, in view of the number of lawyers, rugby enthusiasts, bird-watchers, and assorted kilted Lowlanders from south of Daviot. Was made bearable by the presence of Corriegarth public house which is now, alas, gastrofied. Populated by 'meenisters' (*see below*), schoolteachers, Episcopalians and residents sporting multi-coloured jerseys, binoculars and hiking boots. Used to be home to Inverness Thistle FC ('the Jags', whose Scottish Cup tie against Celtic was once postponed seventeen times owing to inclement weather). The Jags played at Kingsmills Park, outside of which was located the 'Broadstone', the stone marking the boundary of the old Burgh. The stone was once the base for a flagpole: thus 'bored' stone. The park is now full of posh new houses but the stone remains. The 'mill' was established by King Alexander II in 1232, hence the area's regal name, and exists close to the local outdoor 'curling' rink (*see below*).

Culcabock: located at the southern edge of the town. Derives its name – 'the nook of the cheese' – from the Gaelic 'cuil na cabaig'. Why, I have no idea. I do not know anyone who has ever seen, let alone eaten, cheese in this small hamlet. The Highlands' main hospital, Raigmore, built in 1941, can be found here, as can the private Inverness Golf Club (watch out, golfers, when crossing the road that used to be the A9, between the 10th and 11th holes). The Fluke, once a fine old local drinking venue, is the only other attraction but, although still a perfectly decent bar, it lacks the seedy, sleazy camaraderie of yore.

Culloden, Battle of: as most people know, this was the last battle fought on British soil. Culloden (from the Gaelic 'Cuil lodair': 'nook of the marsh') lies four miles south of Inverness. In April 1746 the British Hanoverian army faced Highlanders loyal to the House of Stuart. An oft-quoted line from a US Western movie is 'when the legend becomes fact, print the legend'. The legend of stirring heroic deeds, 'Bonnie' Prince Charlie, 'Over the sea to Skye' and all the rest of it persists to this day. The fact is that this was not a romantic battle between Scots and English, there were as many Highlanders fighting for the government forces as fought for the Jacobites, it was a civil war and a rout, and in its aftermath the Hanoverian leader, the Duke of Cumberland, was culpable of the massacre of hundreds of civilians, many of whom were Hanoverian supporters, and wounded, defenceless Jacobites, thus becoming 'Butcher' Cumberland. The battle cemented British state hegemony over the Highlands and signaled the beginning of the end of the old feudal, Highland way of life. Inverness became a British garrison town, and Charlie boy escaped, due to the courage of many Highlanders, enabling him to return to his life of debauchery in Europe. In a nutshell, that's what happened. (Interestingly, it has been suggested that Inverness's reputation as 'the clearest speakers of English' in Britain dates from this garrison period, although it is difficult to imagine a Gael conversing with a Hanoverian soldier. It is more likely that the 19th-century gradual replacement in the town of the Gaelic tongue by the English language, which the townsfolk mainly learned from books, resulted in this dialect-free clarity.) To discover more about Culloden, visit the impressive tourist centre near the A9 at Drumossie Moor close to where this appalling, needless waste of life occurred. A song entitled *No Gods and Precious Few Heroes* contains the lines: 'Tell me, will we never hear the end / Of poor bloody Charlie at Culloden yet again / When he ran like a rabbit down the glen / Leaving better folk than him to be butchered'. Nevertheless, a stirring legend continues to cast its romantic veil over the truth, a not uncommon feature of Scottish history.

***Curling*:** a curious pastime, which involves rolling a large, round, granite stone of some weight down an ice rink, its progress assisted by 'curlers' brushing its path as it speeds along. Dates from 16th century and is known by devotees as 'the roaring game'. It was originally played exclusively in Scotland and Canada, but its appeal has since spread across a number of other countries, and the 'sport' recently slid into the Olympics. Expertise in the activity increases in direct proportion to the number of drams (*see below*) downed during the match. A team's captain is known as a 'skip', which perhaps refers to his or her adroitness in leaping out of the way of this massive rock as it hurtles past. Can be enjoyed at Kingsmills and Ice Rink.

Dalneigh *(pronounced 'Dalnay'):* the name is Gaelic for 'field of the horses'. There seems to be no etymological reason for this, unless the residents were all jockeys or milkmen. A part of town where very little happens. There are lots of houses, Tomnahurich Cemetery (*see below*) and a school which produces dazzling little inside forwards, who are usually kicked off the pitch by big centre-halves.

Dicht *(pronounced 'dite')*: a word which seems to have ambled its way from the north-east coast of Scotland to Inverness. Its origins are probably mediaeval Dutch, it means 'dense' or 'thick' in German, and it is also the name for a Low Counties board game. It's an Old Scottish word for a digit, while in Inverness it describes the act of giving something or somebody (usually a mucky bairn or 'clart' (*see above*)) a quick flick or a swipe with a cloth to clean them up a bit before visiting their grannie. 'Och, gie yer face a dicht, ye wee clart.' A 'clarty' person's attempts at cleaning are said to be 'gie'ing it a dicht wi' a soor cloot'. No wonder many visitors are bemused by Inverness phrases.

Dirling: probably deriving from the Old English 'thirl' (to 'thrill') and the Old Scots word 'dirl' ('shake' or 'vibrate'). Witness the description of Auld Nick in the grounds of Alloway Kirk in Burns' *Tam O'Shanter*: 'He screw'd the pipes and gart them skirl / Till roof and rafters a' did dirl.' By the time the word had clambered over the Grampians to reach Inverness, 'dirling' had become slightly altered in its meaning. It now carries connotations of 'quivering' or 'tingling', and is often used to describe fingertips after

53

prolonged contact with snow: 'Grannie, ma
fingers are a' dirlin''. 'Well, get oot o' the
snow, then, ye wee bugger'. (Incidentally, the
snowfalls in Inverness can be fearsome and
have been known to cut off the town
completely. Even the snow ploughs give up
the struggle.) 'Dirling' is also often the result
of thinning or topping an iron shot while
playing golf, a popular sport in Inverness,
which possesses four courses, one of which is
a popular stage for the Scottish Open.

'Dooeen' (*equal stress on the two vowels*): a
word which has two meanings. The first is
friendly, as in 'How're ye dooeen?': a polite
request as to your health. The second refers to
a 'belting' (*see above*), and indicates handing
out a severe thrashing: 'I gie'd him a right
dooeen'. Avoid locals who habitually adopt
the latter usage. It's not difficult to tell the
contexts apart.

Dooking (*pronounced 'dookeen'*): often
referred to as 'apple bobbing' south of Daviot,
this is an ancient ritual carried out on
Halloween (31 October), a festival which was
initiated by the ancient Celts and known as
'Samhain' in Gaelic. Young children lean
over a water-filled bucket and try to snatch

floating apples with their mouths. Apples were sacred to the Druids. Some years ago, there were attempts made south of Daviot to ban this harmless fun on the grounds that the custom is 'unhygienic'. Getting your nose wet is unhygienic? And they ask why people live in the Highlands. (*See also 'guising' below*).

***Dottled*:** generally means confused, befuddled and bewildered, and is often applied to those of a certain age. 'Aye, thon old bugger's gey dottled'. It's a word used with affection, tempered with sympathy: it's a cross between 'daft' and 'round the twist'. If you forget your name, put your trousers on the wrong way round or walk into a lamppost, then you're becoming 'dottled'. It's one of those words of Doric or perhaps Caithness origin, which have slipped into the Inverness tongue in a rather absent-minded way. Recently an Aberdeen FC footballer's statement that he was good enough to play for Scotland was described in the press as 'proof that he's dottled'. The highly respected *Child Ballads* collection of the late 1890s includes 'dottled', so the word does have a certain literary pedigree. However, if you're 'dottled', you probably don't know you're 'dottled', so don't worry about it. You'll be perfectly happy.

Dout *(pronounced 'dowt')*: a word one encounters with less frequency in Inverness these days, due to the decline in the smoking habit. Possibly derived from an old English dialect word meaning to extinguish a fire, a 'dout' is a fag which the smoker has 'nipped', ie excised the lit end between thumb and forefinger, leaving both digits a bit 'clarty' (*see above*), leaving what's left ('the dout') for future enjoyment: 'I'll just finish this wee dout and I'll be right wi' ye'. Used to be standard practice in school 'smokers unions' when teachers approached, and also with those short of a few pennies, temporarily, of course. Also, when a bus turned up earlier than you'd expected. 'Ah'll just nip the fag and have the dout in a wee while'. Nothing to do with the Scots' phrase 'I hae ma doots' ('I have my doubts'), but there could be a connection between 'dout' and the Old Scots word 'doit' (an article of little value). 'Gie's a drag o' yer dout, mun…'

Dram: this word can refer to timber from the town of Drammen in Norway. However, in Inverness and Scotland generally it is universally used as a measure of whisky (in Gaelic, 'uisge beatha': the 'water of life'). Also known as a 'wee nip'. Note 'whisky' not 'whiskey'. The measure is specifically one-eighth of a fluid ounce but very few people pay attention to this, as the usual practice is to pour as much as possible into the largest glass one can find. Hardened whisky drinkers used to order quarter-gills, but their evenings were somewhat short in duration. A friend of mine recently asked a 'coast-wester' (*see above*) from Mull how many drams he could extract from a bottle of whisky. After careful consideration, he replied 'Och, about six or seven'. Seasoned whisky imbibers drink the spirit with the same amount of water, in order to bring out the taste and also to make it last longer. Any other mixing agent, such as lemonade or blackcurrant, is strictly forbidden, unless you're a 'wifie' (*see below*) at New Year. Malt whisky was until recently not drunk in quantity as it was distilled for the use of blending, and by itself it was strictly for peasants and 'whinners' (*see below*). Making malt whisky 'posh' was a marketing success story. Excessive intake of this queen of spirits renders one quickly 'blootered' (*see above*). It can also cause serious damage to one's liver and family, but it's a short life so let us enjoy it. 'Do dheagh slainthe': 'your good health'.

Drumnadrochit *(hard 'ch')*: a small village on an inlet on the west bank of Loch Ness, some twelve miles south of the town. A pleasant enough wee place which has given birth to a McGonagall-esque poem, which begins: 'When sore in heart and low in pocket, make your way to Drumnadrochit / Better door ye canna' knock at, than the one in Drumnadrochit'. It gets worse. On a promontory just south of the village sit the ruins of Urquhart Castle (Urquhart derives from the Gaelic 'airchartdan': 'woodside'), once an impressive fortification whose ownership has changed hands several times since the 11th century. John Cobb was killed on the Loch nearby in his powerboat when attempting the world water speed record in the 1930s. Also home to a few hippy communes in the 1960s, when the world was young and love was all around…

Durbs: a pointless activity engaged in by pre-adolescents, usually in school playgrounds, and referred to as 'marbles' south of Daviot. The word may originate from the German 'derb', meaning 'rough' or 'coarse', and that certainly wouldn't surprise me, given the petulant aggression and frequent punch-ups occasioned by 'durbs'. The 'game' consists of throwing onto the ground round coloured bits of glass (the brown ones are known as 'clayacks') and then smashing up the formation with a big 'steely'. The size, and number of victories, of one's steely is a mark of pre-pubescent machismo. Think of 'curling' (*see above*) minus ice, brushes and drams, and indulged in by bairns whose voices have not yet broken, and you're getting the idea.

'een': the Inverness version of the present participle, ie words ending in 'ing'. For instance: 'Ah'm no telleen' ('I choose to remain silent'), 'Aye, it's bucketeen / pisseen doon' ('The rain is rather heavy today'), 'Yer aye hayvureen' ('You persist in obfuscation'), and so on. In common usage throughout the town, although regarded as coarse ('coorse') in the Crown area (*see above*). Examples are many in this volume.

'eeshie noshuns': no, not a character from *Star Wars*, but rather a softly hummed lullaby which Inverness grannies (normally) used to sing to a wee baby in an attempt to cradle the bairn to sleep: 'eeshie noshuns, eeshie no'. Although it's probably influenced by Gaelic mouth music, it's really doggerel, but it was an effective barbiturate substitute. I occasionally used this trick with my little brother and, just as the little darling was about to nod off, I'd drop him on the floor. I was a particularly unpleasant brat as a child, as you can probably tell.

Ferry, Kessock: a part of town, universally known as 'The Ferry', occupying the area between the Merkinch and the Beauly Firth. Named after the fifth century Irish monk St Cessoc who visited these parts before St Columba and who was briefly Scotland's Patron Saint. Used to be the location of the Ferry Service between Inverness and the Black Isle with a boat that could carry two cars and a postie (*see below*). Possesses a dark and sinister reputation – Inverness's equivalent to Tiger Bay or 19th-century Whitechapel. As an example of its internecine volatility, two of its streets - North and South Drive - were referred to by the police as North and South Vietnam. It was also home to a famed athlete from the criminal classes who, it was claimed, could do one hundred meters in three nights, but the Council gradually dispensed with the gas and electric devices and our light-fingered hero disappeared from view.

More recently, the new Kessock Bridge (a thing of majesty, stretching over a thousand metres and opened in 1982 to replace the ferry) has given its name to the derby matches between Dingwall's Ross County and Caley Thistle (*see 'traitors' below*): 'El Kessocko' (the local equivalent of 'El Classico', the not infrequent games between Barcelona and Real Madrid on the Iberian peninsula).

Flog: an interesting word, with several meanings. It is conventionally used to describe a brutal beating with a whip. It also stands for 'fake web log' and 'masturbation' (there is probably a subtle connection here). Its general slang usage throughout the UK is 'to sell' or 'to promote'. However, in Inverness 'flog' means 'to pinch' or 'steal' something. 'I've jist flogged some sweeties from the shop' refers to purloining the confectionery usually from the old Woolworths on the High Street. This appears to be unique to the Inverness area. Some sources cite Australia as the source of the Inverness usage, but I can't understand why or how this interpretation of the word could or would have journeyed from Melbourne to the Merkinch.

Folk Festival: the original Inverness Folk Club was set up in the mid-1960s by the indefatigable Duncan McLennan, an English teacher at the Millburn Academy. Duncan's lugubrious, bearded mien masked a cheerfully ironic wit, an infectious chuckle and a surprising talent for organizing things. He had an extensive knowledge of the embryonic 'folk revival', and he managed to persuade some of the country's finest singers/performers to play in the wee room above the Gellion's Public Bar (*see below*) on Sunday evenings. He also established the annual Folk Festival weekend, showcasing the likes of Archie Fisher, Martin Carthy, Billy Connolly, Gerry Rafferty, Aly Bain, Bert Jansch, Hamish Imlach, Jeannie Robertson, John Renbourn, Barbara Dickson, a young John Martyn, Davy Graham, The Fureys and plenty others. The gigs were held in such venues as the great old bars the Albert and the Northern, Haughdale Hotel (where I once helped Jansch back onto the stool he'd just fallen off), Ice Rink and Town Hall (where Davy Graham was magnificent). Many musicians ended up in the Craigmonie Hotel for extremely 'blootered' musical all-nighters (or 'hootenannies', as the *Sunday Post* might describe them). The Folk Festival became one of the most prestigious events on the British folk music circuit, and is still fondly recalled by all who were fortunate enough to attend and perform.

'Forty Pockets': Inverness has never been never short of worthies or characters, but few became household names. One, however, was 'Forty Pockets', a name used when trying to extract money from your mother ('Who'd ye you think I am? Forty Pockets?'), looking a bit unkempt ('Ye look like Forty Pockets, mun'), and so on. Jimmy 'Forty Pockets' was a luckless indigent from the Merkinch in the 1920s/30s who wore several layers of clothing at once, never mind the weather. Give him some clothes and he'd put them on top of what he was already wearing. He delivered the now-defunct *Football Times* around the Leachkin, to the west of the town. He was a symbol of homelessness in the Inverness area. Recently, a mural appeared on Crown Road (the hill going up from Eastgate to Crown Drive) portraying 'Forty Pockets', though how the artist knew what he looked like is a mystery. Still, it's a memorial to old Inverness (although it looks more like Japan).

'*Four and twenty virgins...* ' came down from Inverness / When the ball was over there were four and twenty less.' Probably more people know about the town from this source – 'The Ball O' Kirriemuir' – than from any other. This is the only clean verse in an extended, filthy sing-a-long, to which people keep adding even bawdier verses. Seemingly first appeared as a rugby song ('rugby' being defined as 'lawyers running into each other'). The mystery is how they managed to find all these virgins in a place like Inverness, a town not renowned for its coy modesty. 'Yer aye droppeen yer drawers, Morag...'

Gaelic *(Highland Gaelic, 'Gaidhlig', pronounced 'gallic' not 'gaylic'*): descended from the Old Irish Celtic language, Gaelic gradually became the language and culture of the Picts, and by the 12th century was the main language of what is now Scotland. English (albeit in its various 'Scots' dialects), however, assumed dominance in much of the country over the following centuries, and Gaelic withdrew to the Highlands and Islands. After the battle of Culloden (*see above*), the Gaelic language was outlawed, and speakers were often persecuted by the British state. It is now spoken mainly in the Hebrides but has recently been granted 'equal respect' (whatever that means) alongside English by the Scottish Parliament. To describe someone as 'having the Gaelic' means that he or she can converse in the Gaelic tongue. Many Highland road and venue signs are now in both Gaelic and English, although it is a mystery how local government officers knew, for instance, the Gaelic word for an airport (Dalcross is signposted 'Port-Adhair'). BBC Alba is a Gaelic TV station, available across the UK, and probably also to the homesick 'cheuchter' community worldwide. I recall recently watching on my computer in London a Scottish Premier League football match on BBC Alba in the company of an American, a Frenchwoman and a Serb, with the Gaelic match commentary excitedly enunciated in an Aberdonian accent. Multinational we may all now be, but it is heartening to see that strenuous efforts are continually being made to preserve the ancient historic tongue of the Highland Gaels. And how many of you knew they had airports in those days?

Gadgie: a term which derives from the travelling people, and is the 'tinker' (*see below*) word for a 'non-tinker'. Widely used outside the travelling community in the same sense as 'bodach' (*see above*), ie a mate or colleague, and usually applied with a degree of affection. The female equivalent of 'gadgie' is the rarely heard 'manashee'. The etymology of 'gadgie' is obscure. Could be from 'gadhelic' (pertaining to Gaeldom), 'gadder' (to be on the go to little purpose) or 'gadabout' (one who flits about in social activity). I would be surprised if it emanates from 'Gad' (head of one of the twelve tribes of Israel), but you never know. It's probably a mixture of the first three. 'Gadgie coff', often heard in the far reaches of the Black Isle to the north, is even more perplexing, but means the same thing. 'Coff' comes from 'cove', and may be added to give the word a poetic edge. Or it may have a link with the Arabic 'coffle' ('a train of slaves chained together'), which could explain Ross County.

Gellions: a legendary bar located on Bridge Street, the sloping road down to the main bridge, known as the 'new bridge': there have been several over the centuries (*see 'Ness Bridge' below*). The name 'Gellions' comes from the Gaelic 'Gellian', meaning 'servant of St John' (no, I'm afraid I'm not any the wiser, either), and was famed for the variety, eccentricities and good-humoured delinquency of its clientele. The bar staff (hello, Monty) had a reputation for caustic humour and witty put-down lines. They were friendly people but they had to adopt a defence mechanism to handle some of the 'heiders', or somewhat unruly customers, they were obliged to serve. Scotland's great national poet (after Burns) William McGonagall visited the Gellions, which could go some way to explaining his extraordinary 'poetry' (being 'blootered' *(see above)* is not regarded as a stimulus to subtle poetic meter and versification). Inverness Folk Club began life above the Public Bar. Hand-over-ear folk singers, often librarians, had to compete with the cheerful racket from downstairs. The Gellions was an assembly point for the town's younger 'glitterati' (or 'skyveen wasters' as they were fondly known).

Gey (pronounced 'guy', with the 'u' tending to 'i' in 'ice'): an adverb of universal usage in Inverness. 'Aye, yer lookin' gey pleased wi' yersel''. Means 'fairly' via 'considerably' to 'very', depending on the context and emphasis. Seemingly derives from the early 18th-century English 'gay' (although the connection escapes me), and made its way to Inverness via Northumbria and Old Scots.

'It's gey dreich the now' ('the weather is pretty miserable today'). 'Fair' is similar to 'gey': 'Aye, thon wee ben's a fair walk' ('that hill is some distance away').

Greet: does not necessarily mean a hearty welcome: it depends on the context. The usage to which I here refer derives from the Norse 'grata': to weep, and means to sob uncontrollably, often at some imagined slight. Contains a pejorative element if you're a 'mannie' (*see below*), as in 'stop yer greetin', ye wee lassie': two insults in one phrase.

Groick: this could be of Germanic or Gaelic origin, or just made up by someone who once misread Tolkien. A 'groick' is a clumsy, dithering, clueless individual who keeps getting things wrong. The word, however, is usually delivered with a degree of sympathy, and signifies exasperation rather than anger. 'Och, yer just a groick' is utilised when, for instance, you've forgotten to buy some butter when you went for the 'messages' (*see below*). It indicates mild frustration, so don't worry about it. It doesn't mean you've poisoned your grannie. We're all 'groicks' at some point or another.

Guddling: hanging around doing nothing, while giving the impression of being deep in productive thought. 'Och, I'm jist guddling'. Occasionally involves 'blethers' (*see above*) but can normally be attributed to sheer laziness or thinking about where your next pint's coming from. 'Guddling' (or 'tickling') also refers to snatching trout, or even salmon, from a river with your bare hands, something of a rare and an acquired skill.

Guising (*pronounced 'gyseen'*): another Halloween tradition (*see 'dooking' above*), based on Druidic practices. Children dressed up and visited nearby houses, and had to recite a poem or perform a song to receive an apple or sweetie. Witches' hats were common wear, and faces were often blackened. The Druids used wood ash. Today it's known as 'trick or treat' and the little darlings expect a wee giftie for simply turning up. Only reward them if they can recite 'Tam O'Shanter' in its entirety (and with Burns' words correctly pronounced).

Gurneen: probably originating from 'gurning' in the north of England, it describes a sour-faced, miserable and complaining disposition, therefore very common in

Inverness. Often in evidence the morning after being 'blootered' (*see above*). 'Yer aye gurneen, Donnie. If the wind changes ye'll stay that way.' 'Ach, haud yer wheesht ('do be quiet'). Nothing that a couple of drams canna' fix.' Given the prevailing humour of the local inhabitants, 'gurneen' is a frequent phenomenon, at least until the bars have opened.

Haddie: although the hoi polloi of Inverness are generally tolerant of harmless misdemeanours, they are not slow to express their opinions when they perceive what they believe to be crass incompetence. There are several epithets available for such occasions, one of the most dismissive being 'haddie'. An example: 'How did ye manage to miss thon shot? A wee bairn could've bumped it in with its erse. Whit a haddie'. There is no response to this. You can't really argue that 'I'm no' a haddie', as you'll then look an even bigger haddie. It's more degrading than being called a 'lammie' (*see below*) but you just have to accept it. The term almost certainly derives from the king of the seas, the haddock, known locally as a 'Finnan haddie' ('Finnan' being a corruption of Findhorn, a wee seaside village in the dark lands east of Nairn, which is full of hippies and clueless dinghy sailors but is also a supplier of some fine haddock). Fish are completely hopeless at everything except being fish, so the implications of being called a 'haddie' are clear.

Haugh, the *('gh' as in pre-expectorant clearing of throat)*: originates either from the Old English 'heolh' meaning 'a low-lying meadow by the side of a river' or the Gaelic 'an talchan', meaning much the same. The Haugh is the area stretching from the foot of the Castle (*see above*) to Bellfield Park with its tennis courts and other amenities beside the River Ness. The Haugh Bar was afforded a similar heroic, dignified status in Inverness folklore as the Black Bull (*see above*) across the river, and dainty little hotels line the riverside road. In the 17th century the Haugh was home to a popular horseracing track, and was later the site of a brewery. A struggle up the wee 'brae' (*see above*) known as the 'Godsies' (the original path having been laid out by an English landowner, Captain Godsman) takes you up to the bourgeois security of the Crown area.

Havers (*pronounced 'hayvurs'*): again, heard south of Daviot. An adaptation of 'havering' ('hayvureen'): to talk rubbish. Interestingly, used most frequently by grannies and aunties when one is attempting to embellish one's achievements: 'I've never heard such a load of old havers'. Also used to describe the meaningless utterances of imbibers of certain chemical substances. A useful term to employ when one disagrees with anything or anyone.

Heavy, pint of: a phrase once used throughout Scotland and, as one might expect, it was particularly common in Inverness. If you're standing at a bar and hear someone ask for a 'pint of heavy', don't be alarmed. This is not a macho, muscle-building request for a half-litre of cement, nor is it an invitation to indulge in arm wrestling with the barman or a quaint 'Highland tradition' such as 'tossing the caber'. Indeed, even 'wifies' (*see below*) have been known to ask for a 'pint of heavy' in public houses. The word simply means flat, 'bitter' beer, of the sort they drink in faraway lands, like England. 'Heavy', at between 3.5-4.5% abv (alcohol by volume), is stronger than 'light' but not up there with the strongest: 'export'. Until very recently, 'heavy' was the standard beer of choice among the local drinking classes (which consists of just about everybody), but it has now virtually disappeared and has ceded its dominance to trendier, unpronounceable Germanic-sounding bevvies. Occasionally, you may hear a slurred demand for a 'half and half', a half-pint of 'heavy' and a large dram of whisky. These are usually serious drinkers, so keep away from them as the evening progresses: no good will come of your attempt to engage them in polite conversation. Also, never ask for 'a pint of your finest ale, my good man', as someone may take a swing at you for being a 'sassenach' (*see below*). But it must be said that, even if you're sitting quietly minding your own business, someone may decide to take a swing at you: so avoid giving him an excuse. However, set your mind at rest. Such unprovoked aggression from an inhabitant of Inverness is most unusual, unless you happen to come from Nairn (*see below*).

Hielan' dancing: I still cringe when I remember being forced to learn this stuff in the weeks leading up to the school Christmas Dance. This is yet another example of 'kilt and kailyard' (cod-Scottish) Victoriana. The 'laddies' wore 'kilts' (*see below*) and the 'lassies' were arrayed in flimsy, floor-length dresses. The idea was to fling oneself around the dance floor in absurd contortions while trying to keep up with 'Scottish' country music. The 'dances' included Highland Fling, Highland Schottische (a form of polka which originated in Bohemia, of all places), Strip the Willow (really), Dashing White Sergeant and Gay Gordons (the last two having nothing to do with sexual preference, although...). I am unable to continue, due to sheer embarrassment. Was a regular component of the excruciating 'White Heather Club' ('White Blether Club' or 'Why Bother Club', as I called it), a weekly TV programme which, older readers may remember, was presented by a kilted bletherskite named Andy Stewart. It was truly awful and presented a view of a Highlands which had never existed. 'With the hills of hame before us, and the purple of the heather...' Who permitted this torture to be broadcast?

Highland Capital: a term often applied to Inverness, but a misleading honorific. Inverness is by some distance the largest conurbation in the Highland Region and is the main service and administrative centre, but it is not formally a 'capital' of anything. Also, given the cultural and linguistic diversity of its inhabitants, it could also be argued that it is not, other than geographically, part of the 'Highlands'. However, 'Highland Capital' helps attract visitors, fills a few hotel rooms and makes everyone feel good, so perhaps we should leave it as it is. It does no harm and conveys a useful, if spurious, authority.

Hockmagandie: 'a wee bit of hockmagandie' means an illicit or casual romantic dalliance with a member of the opposite sex (usually). No obvious Gaelic connection, so must be somehow onomatopoeic in origin, though that's also difficult to understand. Probably based on some other word uttered when 'blootered' (*see above*) and has stood the test of time. I suspect there are several other words with just such a genesis.

Hogmajerick: this is also a difficult word to unravel. It sounds like a combination of four different languages, and can be loosely defined as a 'loveable rascal'. However, its meaning depends on the tone in which it is uttered. It is best to assume it is a mildly exasperated criticism, and behave accordingly. It is, however, a useful word to employ, as no one quite knows what 'hogmajerick' means and therefore cannot deny being one. Good for ending arguments.

Inversneck: Inverness's equivalent to New York's 'the Big Apple', although lacking the latter's preening grandeur. Often shortened to 'Sneckie' (If an Invernessian can make a word shorter...). A term of comparatively recent origin describing the Highland Capital (*see above*), from an inhabitant's perspective. It may have first appeared when an Invernessian forgot where he lived and came up with 'Inversneck' as the best he could manage in the circumstances. This is perfectly possible. The Inversnecky is also the name of a café on Aberdeen beach, which was named in honour of music hall performer Harry Gordon, known as 'The Laird of Inversnecky'.

'It's worse yer improveen': a classic, and the Inverness equivalent of the 'tall poppy' syndrome. Nothing you may achieve, no matter how important or significant, can be acknowledged without a reminder of your fallibility. Despite its semantic illogicality, this is a real compliment. It's usually accompanied by a knowing but friendly grin and a nudge of the elbow. You may be a smart arse, but you're still a 'bodach' (*see above*). Accept this apparently grudging praise with some grace, as it's as good as you'll get.

Jar: a receptacle, naturally, but a word also used in Inverness to deliver a sharp and forceful reminder: 'Ah've jist jarred Wullie about thon fiver I gie'd him last week'. The word appears in conversation when least expected, the better to convey its impact. To be 'jarred' is to suffer a stern but deserved rebuke: harsh, but just.

Jouping *(pronounced 'joopeen'):* origin uncertain, but most probably from the French 'jeu' ('play'). This is described by school children as 'joopeen off', or absenting oneself, from school to make one's day more enjoyable. This was often spent in Hunter's Snooker Hall on the High Street (sixteen full-size tables!), now, alas, long gone. Jouping normally begins with phoney morning coughing in an attempt to fool one's mother, rarely a successful tactic. Forging a sick note is tricky, as teachers are not as stupid as they look. And, when 'joopeen', don't forget to take off your school blazer when you enter a bar.

'Keep a calm sooch' *(hard 'ch'):* employed, normally by parents and grannies (who are never far from the action), when bairns are over-excited, rushing around or otherwise excessively exuberant. 'Sooch' derives from the Gaelic word 'sough': an unsettling murmur or a sinister rustling, usually applied to the wind, which is omnipresent to varying degrees in the Highlands. 'Keep a calm sooch' should be expressed in a reassuring, soothing manner, as it means 'take it easy', 'slow down' or 'don't get so worked up'.

Kaylee: Not the pert-bummed wee Oz lassie, but the English pronunciation of the Gaelic word 'ceilidh', a derivation of the Old Irish 'cele', or 'companion'. Originally a clan social gathering, featuring bardic storytelling and versifying, it now refers to an evening of 'Scottish' dancing, eating (usually mashed-up bits of dead sheep), drinking ('just a small one, then, Fiona's driving tonight') and what passes for music of the Hielan' persuasion. If preceded by the suggestion 'fancy a wee bit of a piss-up when the Phoenix shuts?' this usually promises an entertaining, 'blootered' (*see above*), musical evening, or a *real* ceilidh, in store: a ceilidh should be a spur-of-the-moment decision to get completely wasted. However, if you receive a card embossed with the words 'Mr and Mrs

Torquil McTavish invite you to a Ceilidh…'
then avoid this at all costs. Jump under a bus,
insult a brawny coast-wester's female
companion: anything other than sitting in
some tartan-bedecked room, watching
disbelievingly as a few recent immigrants
from Esher prance around in an 'eightsome
reel'. A ceilidh has been appropriated as part
of 'authentic Highland culture', and any
sensible bodach, if you can find one, will
recoil in horror at the prospect of becoming
involved (unless he knows the accordionist,
who normally has a bottle hidden away).
Escape this lunacy by saying you have to
catch the last bus to Clachnaharry. They
won't know where this is (they probably don't
know what a bus is). There is no need to
encourage the dominance of tartan
teuchterdom: it'll happen anyway. (*See
'Hielan' dancing' above.*)

Kennedy, Calum: a 'cheuchter' (*see above*)
and a popular chanteur in Inverness and south
of Daviot. He was no doubt a decent,
charming man, and he was generally regarded
as one of the finest singers of his time.
However, in his dress he personified, as did
'The White Heather Club' (*see 'Hielan'
dancing' above*), the most shameful

representation of faux-Highland culture invented by Walter Scott and his Victorian aristocratic chums. Along with his intricately patterned kilt, Calum usually wore a freshly ironed white frilly shirt and bowtie under his black tailored evening jacket, the outfit finished off with gleaming pumps. Can you imagine yourself cowering at the foot of a glowering, Highland mountain in the wind and rain, hearing the ferocious, blood-chilling Gaelic war cries as the enemy clan charged down in your direction, armed with their claymores and targes (small shields)? As they emerged through the mist, however, you would be more likely to die from laughter than from cold steel, if they were attired in Calum's preferred mode of leisure wear. Which brings me to 'kilts'…

Kilt: do not wear this item of clothing under the impression that it is an essential component of ancient Highland clan history. It is not. 'Kilts' were originally loose, plaid garments which were patchily dyed in various colours, with one end slung over the shoulder, and were the standard dress for men. There were no particular colours claimed by different clans: they just employed whatever dye was handy. The probable origin of the word (several origins have been suggested) is the Old Danish 'kilte' meaning 'to tuck up'. The lack of restrictive leggings made it easier for Highlanders to scramble over the rocks, and thereby escape with the coos they'd just nicked from the Hanoverian estates south of Daviot. 'Tartan', however, is a 19th-century invention, along with Balmoral Castle, the 'noble' clan chief (who often lived in England or France) and all the other Victoriana, designed to get tourists to spend their money here rather than somewhere else. However, women apparently find men in kilts attractive ('aye, he's got no' a bad pair o' legs for an old bodach'), and therefore one should not be too dogmatic in one's pious observations, as this could be an opportunity...

Kirk: although the phrase 'beam me aboard, Scotty' is the normal non-Scottish reaction when hearing the word 'Kirk', this word was the official title of the Church of Scotland until the 17th century, and is still used throughout Scotland to describe a Presbyterian place of worship: except, that is, in the Inverness area, where the English word 'church' is the universally preferred term. 'Kirk' and 'church' stem from the same root, the Ancient Greek word 'kyriakon', and they are useful identifiers as to the origins of your partner in conversation. If you are talking in Inverness with a Scottish person and this person casually mentions 'kirk' as a fun Sunday relaxation, then it's a safe bet that he or she hails from the Saxon lands south of Daviot or the Doric darkness to the east of Nairn (*see below*). You are almost certainly not talking to an Invernessian. The word 'church' reflects not only the 17th-century Cromwellian (*see 'Citadel' above*) and 18th-century Hanoverian garrison occupations of the town, but also its origins as a Catholic settlement and its varied and various religious influences over the centuries. 'Kirk' is normally used in Inverness solely with reference to the Kirk Session, the court of elders in the local Presbyterian congregations. Also, every September the town rings to the skirlin' o' the bagpipes when councilors from Highland Council, stumble *en masse* down to the Old High Church in a quest for spiritual approbation in a ceremony known as the 'Kirking of the Council'. This pointless meander has been going on for 400 years and, gazing around at the decrepitude of some of the participants, one could be excused for thinking that some of the original councilors are still taking part.

Laldy: another of those words of baffling origin, but one which is used widely in Inverness and south of Daviot. Most often heard in the phrase 'gie it some laldy', meaning 'use everything in your power to achieve the desired result' or 'just gie' it a good wallop'. Often directed at centre forwards in front of goal: 'och, gie it some laldy, ye big midden'. It also, like so many Invernessian words, carries implications of impending doom, usually at the hands of one's male parent: 'I'll gie thon wee bugger some laldy when he gets home the night'. Possibly originates from the travelling people, but has also been suggested as deriving from an old Scots word for a 'whip', which makes sense.

Lambie (or 'lammie'): a baby sheep and, by extrapolation, also a censorious epithet applied to a 'mannie' (*see below*) who has just done something naive and stupid. Was often used in local snooker halls when an easy pot was missed: 'och, yer just a lammie'. Caley Thistle (*see 'traitors' below*) 'fans' often bellow this term – 'Lammie!' – in unison when, as is normally the case, their centre-forward misses an open goal. 'Lammie' throws a question mark over one's masculinity, but it's still not as bad as being called a 'whinner' (*see below*). Few insults are worse than this.

Lander on the lug: 'If ye dinnae behave yersel', ye'll get a lander on the lug' was a statement of intent from parents or grannies designed to cow hyperactive 'wee bairns' (young children). A 'lander' is a 'skelp' (slap), while a 'lug' is an ear. So the meaning is clear. Such a 'lander' was rarely delivered. The threat was usually sufficient to achieve its purpose. Yet another Invernessian phrase implying violent activity, but in a surprisingly affectionate way.

Law and Order: The Inverness police are honest, incorruptible, patient, pleasant and decent public servants, who assist old 'wifies'(*see below*) across the road, help the traffic move when road lights malfunction, tell off wee boys who cycle on the pavement, and are generally a shining example to us all. Well, two of them are: the rest are not quite so PC Murdoch. Although it is cruelly suggested that they haven't solved a murder since the Glencoe Massacre of 1692, they can be assiduous in their pursuit of the Inverness criminal classes (also numbered on two fingers of the hand). Essentially, they are the same as police forces everywhere although, unlike their counterparts south of Daviot, they are never referred to as 'polis', a word which we educated Invernessians use for describing an ancient Greek city-state. They are normally addressed as 'Sorry, officer', 'Honest, Jimuck, it'll no' happen again' or 'He had it comin', the wee whinner''. They labour under the unfortunate nickname of 'hornies', a word which has its origin in the travelling people's nickname for the Devil. The travellers also call them 'ploops', but better leave that one. One of our contributors witnessed a mass 'boorach' (*see above*) at a local private dwelling, and was told by an observer "the hornies arrived and threw an accordion around the building": an unusual means of social control, but perhaps the boys in blue felt that the soothing tones of a eightsome reel might calm down the participants. However, don't mess with the 'hornies' and, as a rule, they won't mess with you.

Loch Ness: the inventor of the mythical 'Nessie' deserves the Celtic Flaming Cross Medal. The Loch Ness Monster is a marketing triumph to rank alongside the yeti. (Incidentally, several yeti-like creatures appear to inhabit Inverness, but closer inspection reveals them to be 'coast-westers' (*see above*): this is a feeble attempt at a joke, by the way, as the last thing I need is a 'kick in the erse' from an offended 'coast-wester'.) An even more brilliant idea was to suggest an underground tunnel between Loch Ness and the North Sea: a subway for the monster. Better still was to create the legend of St Columba in the 6th century AD facing down a 'sea monster'. However, to stand on Dores 'beach' (nine miles south-west of Inverness) and gaze south down the sixty-odd miles of the Great Glen (in Gaelic 'An Gleann Mor') is to witness nature at its most rugged and splendid. The loch is at least 800 feet deep (because of the underwater overlapping rock shelves it has been difficult to discover the exact depth by sonar means) so don't even think about swimming in it. It is freezing. (*See also 'Caledonian Canal' and 'Drumnadrochit' above.*)

Loon: a word of Scandinavian origin for diving, fish-eating birds, which originated in the lands east of Nairn (*see below*), otherwise known as The Lowlands, to describe young lads. Has filtered its way into local usage. Rarely employed in its south of Daviot sense of 'crazy': rather it is an affectionate, friendly term. The female equivalent is 'quine', the original meaning of which was 'prostitute' but now simply refers to an unmarried young woman. Be careful, though.

MacBeth: ' will all great Neptune's ocean wash this blood clean from my hand?'(after he had murdered Duncan). Duncan's body is reputed to have been buried close to King Duncan's Well, a spring located in Culcabock (*see above*). Although most of the action in Shakespeare's 'Scottish Play' takes place in the area which is now Perthshire (the Bard's grasp of Scottish geography may have been less than entirely accurate), MacBeth had a castle in Inverness, most likely on the hill in the Crown area (*see above*) overlooking the old Inverness Royal Academy Playing Fields. He was, in the 11th century, Mormaer (regional commander) of Moray, and his Gaelic name was Mac Bethad Mac Findlaich (no wonder he shortened it). He was, memorably in the words of the Second Witch, Thane of Cawdor: 'All hail to thee, Thane of Cawdor'. Cawdor is just a few miles to the east of Inverness, and the existing Cawdor Castle is built on the ruins of an earlier fortification, probably that of MacBeth.

Mackles: one of Inverness's 'characters'. 'Mackles' was a friendly, eccentric individual normally dressed in a red blazer and, like many Invernessians, fond of the odd dram or, on occasion, a few more. He had a fine singing voice which could charm the Gellions Back Bar (*see above*) – not an easy thing to do – with his misty-eyed crooning of old Highland ballads into an empty pint glass. A Merkincher (*see below*) and Clach supporter, he organised penalty shoot-outs involving local kids during half time at home games. The kids had a great time although Mackles was known to fall over before making contact with the ball. He became friendly with Billy Connolly who used to visit Inverness for the annual Folk Festival (*see above*) in the 1960s. Billy admired Mackles as a singer, a character and a raconteur, and the two of them, so alike in many ways, kept in touch for several years. Stories, nay legends, abound about this occasionally hapless, often chaotic but always good-natured and well-meaning man, who symbolised the essentially decent spirit of an old Inverness culture, which was gradually evolving into anodyne, consumerist 'modernity'. He was thrawn (*see below*), cheerfully unconventional in his behaviour and defiant in his refusal to succumb to stultifying conformity: an example to us all. He died several years ago, and one of his old buddies played Mackles' 'moothie' (mouth organ) over his coffin at the packed funeral. Half time at the Clach Park has never been the same since Mackles wandered off gamely into the hereafter.

Maggot: nothing to do with 'midgie' (*see below*), nor is it the 17th-century dance of the same name. 'Maggot' is the stretch of land between the old swimming baths on the River Ness and the Black Bridge, a space once used for the washing and drying of clothes. The word is a corruption of St Margaret's Chapel, which used to stand on the site. It is also where the 'wifies' (*see below*) carried their menfolk on their backs to their boats, a phenomenon which is replicated today when they drag their menfolk home at closing time. It's heart-warming to observe the continuance of old traditions.

Mannie: a cross between 'bodach' and 'bachle' (*see above*) but implies less intimacy than either. The word suggests a one-off encounter: 'och, I met a mannie in the street once…' For some reason he's always 'wee'. I've never heard tell of a 'big mannie'. Curiously, the plural is not 'men' but 'mannies'. 'See all thon wee mannies…'

Mart: up until the 1990s there was a lively weekly cattle and livestock market or 'Mart' held on the north side of Millburn Road near to the Eastgate 'retail experience' shopping wonderland, which today apparently caters to 'the largest shopping catchment area in Europe' (well, perhaps in a geographical sense), and Falcon Square, with its new 'mercat cross'. When this new consumers' temple was being developed, one of the old buildings was demolished and rebuilt stone by original stone. Unfortunately for traditionalists, it faced in a different direction to the previous building in order to fit into the new layout, and is now occupied by local retailers Pizza Express and Laura Ashley. The Mart was then converted into a 'super' Mart, first becoming Safeways and now Morrisons. Before all this 'modernisation' occurred, Hamilton's Auction Mart, for such was its name, used to be jammed with trailers, land rovers and cattle trucks, and reverberated to the sounds of 'mooing', 'neighing' and much cursing. The coos were herded in to Inverness from the surrounding hinterland and were temporarily quartered in the large field between Damfield Road and the

8th fairway of the golf course at Culcabock (*see above),* before they were marched through the Kingsmills area of the Crown (*see above*) and down Stephens Brae to the Mart for their day of judgement. In the 1950s a disaffected coo, named Sally, did a runner from her moorings at the Mart, veered onto Eastgate, clattered past four now sadly defunct hostelries, skidded into Hamilton Street, entered a dairy, lumbered up the stairs to the first floor and fell through to the floor beneath. The coo, beaming with delight at her escapade and unharmed by her dash for freedom, was escorted back to the Mart by her proud owner. In the first week of July there was held a Wool Fair day, where ponies and horses were sold by auction, and sometimes 'hot shod' by the blacksmith at the nearby 'smiddy' (an Old Scots term for the English 'smithy') while the animals' owners watched. In the years before all this frenetic activity began, the Mart was marshland susceptible to flooding, and contained a stagnant pool known as Loch Gorm (Gaelic for 'the turquoise loch': what a misnomer), a name also adopted by a grand wee bar along the road. It was drained in the mid-18th century (the marsh not the bar although, in the case of the latter, it was not for lack of trying).

Meenister: an ordained minister within the Presbyterian or Free Church (*for 'Wee Free' see below*). Of similar status to an Episcopalian rector or a Roman Catholic priest, both of which are in a minority in Inverness, but everyone gets on fine with each other. A 'meenister' can range in character from the unctuous to the hearty, and generally enjoys a high social ranking. 'Och, the meenister's comin' roond for tea. Better get oot yer grannie's best cups and saucers.' Wears a white rounded collar, so easily spotted and avoided, although usually up for the 'crack' (*see above*) particularly after a few 'drams' (*see above*).

Meeshahanagit-trala: a word which sounds like a combination of Ancient Hebrew and Swahili, but which is uttered, along with a shaking of the head, a sigh and a lifting of the eyes, to indicate total exasperation. It is often occasioned by having to listen to an excess of 'havers' (*see above*) or excuses for one's aberrant behaviour. Its etymology is lost in the mists of Gaelic time. It can describe one's reaction to the futility of existence as much as to leaving dirty footprints in your grannie's front room. There is absolutely no response to this existential rebuke, other than to shake your head sympathetically and agree.

Merkinch *(a soft 'ch', unusually)*: the oldest part of Inverness and, in the eyes of many, it remains the romantic heart of the town. Derives from the Gaelic 'Marc-innis' ('horse island'). Located across the Black Bridge over the River Ness and facing the once-busy Harbour in the Longman industrial area, it was an industrial, shipbuilding centre from the 11th century and a flat island until comparatively recently in its history. Indeed, a 'merk' is a measure of land which is the size of a small island. Clachnacuddin FC (*see above*) is a cherished local institution, and Clach v Caley games were fiercely contested territorial derbies. Once the only genuinely working-class area in the town, but many of the old streets and houses have been demolished in the name of 'progress'. Was once populated by rogues, working girls, ne'er-do-wells, vagabonds and hard-working, decent people, but now becoming gentrified. 'Oh look, darling, we can see the Black Isle from the lounge window. How charming'. Life is unfair.

Messages: has nothing to do with communication, unless the context so permits.

'I'm just going for the messages' does not refer to sneaking out to collect spy documents in pre-designated locations. It means going to the 'shops', of which there used to be a good number until supermarkets arrived. Can also include the shopkeeper's name: 'I'm off to Jimmy Chisholm's for the messages'. The term is mysterious in origin, but possibly derives from the message boys who delivered the groceries to wealthier parts of town.

Midgies: do not visit the West coast of Scotland in August, particularly if you are camping in a tent. You run a serious risk of being tormented to your wits' ends by 'midgies' (from the ancient Greek 'myia', meaning 'fly'): tiny, gnat-like insects which gather by the thousand expressly and deliberately to inflict bites on your body. Lighting a fire and chain smoking help to keep them at bay, but they'll get you in the end. Waving your arms about only attracts them, as they probably think you want to be their friend. 'Midgies' have been known to break up not only holidays but also marriages. A folk tale persists that 'midgies' are the finely chopped but very much alive remains of a man-eating giant. You should escape them in Inverness, although a few midgie colonies exist in the area. A certain reclusive character nicknamed Dave the Cave used to live near Dores on the northeast corner of Loch Ness just a few miles from Inverness. When he moved further south down the loch to Foyers to build himself a wooden hermitage, he became known as Dancing With Midgies. Just watch out for these troublesome beasties.

Mingin': nothing to do with the Chinese Ming dynasty. From the Old Scots' word 'ming', a bad smell. 'Mingin'' is commonly used to describe a disgusting odour ('aye, it was fair mingin''), or can be applied to someone of questionable personal or hygenic habits: 'he/she was a right minger'. Avoid using the word in the hearing of the person concerned, as it is deeply insulting. Refer to the victim by another term of abuse: there are plenty of them.

Movie memories (cinemas, the 'flicks' or the 'pictures' (pronounced 'pickchurs')): before the arrival of the 'multiplex cinema' (a sure indication of cultural imperialism and the general dumbing down of one's critical faculties), the Crown area (*see above*) 'film society' (with subtitles so one can appreciate fully the absence of artistic merit of a few pretentious movies), and the justifiably renowned Eden Court complex, there existed in the town four 'cinemas': the Palace, Empire, Playhouse and La Scala. The Palace was opened in 1938 beside the river on Huntly Street, had room for 1200 moviegoers and a grand restaurant, and was converted to a bingo hall in 1963. It is now a Premier Inn (and a very comfortable one, at that). The Empire, on Academy Street, was built as the Central Hall Picture House as early as 1912, was converted to a theatre in 1936 (when it was renamed the Empire), and is now, sadly, demolished. The Playhouse (born 1922 and destroyed by fire in 1972) stood near to the 'Eastgate Shopping Experience' (*see 'Mart' above*), next to a kiltie shop. This was the posher of the two remaining cinemas, had its own restaurant and showed serious and important movies such as 'The Sound of Music' and 'The King and I'. It even contained toilets for the use of patrons, as well as selling ice-lollies and Butterkist. This was the favoured venue of teachers, Calum Kennedy fans (*see above*) and meenisters (*see above*), but not Wee Free meenisters, as it smacked far too much of enjoyment. Centre-halves, whinners and bodachs (*see below and above*), however, preferred the rougher cultural experience of the La Scala (another early picture palace, built in

1913 and still screening movies until 2001),
which was located on the junction of Academy
Street and Strothers Lane, close to Farraline Park
bus station and handy for a quick getaway after
one had nicked the evening's takings. Although
it fell slightly short of the cultural grandeur of its
Milan namesake, La Scala compensated for this
with its Saturday morning 'matinees'
(pronounced 'mattnees, mun') which promoted,
in return for a nine pence entrance fee, films
aimed at the edification of young hooligans, of
whom there were more than several in Inverness.
Most of these badly-behaved brats (among
whom, sadly, I count myself) sat in the seats
above the stalls and spent the morning dropping
ice-cream and sweeties onto the heads of those
below, while evading the clutches of the
hilariously-clad 'Torchy', the usher and
commissionaire. There was usually a Look at
Life ('and here we are in Venice, with its
beautiful gondolas… and there's another
gondola… and, yes, another boring gondola'), a
cartoon and a cowboy serial, often The Lone
Ranger ('Hi-Ho, Silver, and away, mun'). The
first few bars of God Save The Queen at the end
were enough to evacuate the place with some
speed, the young ne'er-do-wells normally
heading off to start a 'boorach' (*see above*) at the
Eastgate chip shop or visit their grannies to

borrow money to go to the afternoon's Clach game. These venues have all succumbed to the crumbling cinema reel of time, but the highly praised Eden Court Centre proudly continues the local Inverness 'flicks' tradition: to the extent that, in homage to our filmic history, they name their two cinemas... the La Scala and the Playhouse.

Mrs Rose: a peculiar acknowledgement used by ladies of a certain vintage when addressing each other. I use 'Mrs Rose' as an example, as my grannie used to say 'Mrs Rose is coming to tea'. Mrs Rose would arrive and say 'Hello, Mrs MacWilliam' and, so far as I could eavesdrop, they never used each other's Christian names. Perhaps they never knew them, although they had been regular co-visitors for countless years. Strange, but perhaps they thought that was what constituted politeness. (Her first name, by the way, was Ida: Mrs Rose's, that is. To me, my grannie didn't have a first name. She was just 'Grannie'.)

Nairn (pronounced 'Nern' not 'Nayrn'): a small town, named after the Pictish word for 'stream', fifteen miles east of Inverness. The road to Nairn contains 'the Nairn straight', six miles of completely straight tarmac, intersected by the Inverness-Nairn railway line. (An apocryphal, if perfectly believable, story is that a speeding motorcyclist once failed to notice that the level crossing bar was down and had his head sliced off. Best not to dwell on this.) Passes Dalcross Airport (from Gaelic 'dealg an rois': 'prickly wood') from where Dan Air (known as 'Dan Dare') inaugurated cheap flights. Nairn is schizophrenic: on its west side live the posh, upper-classes (for a lyrical, evocative account of growing up in this area in the early 20th century, read David Thomson's book *Nairn: In Darkness and Light*); while on the east is Fishertoun, home to the fishermen and working classes, caravan site and huge, sandy but dangerously unpredictable tidal beach. Used to be Inverness holiday resort during the 'Trades Fortnight' when businesses closed down for two weeks. Boasts a splendid old harbour and two championship golf courses. Interesting to note that this is where the accent changes, quite dramatically and noticeably, from the lilting, Gaelic-influenced tongue to the harsh, Doric tones of the Lowlands. The town's inhabitants are universally known as 'nairnucks'.

Neaps: or 'neeps' are Swedish turnips. Nothing to do with a neap tide. Simply a lazy way of saying 'turnip', although neaps' are usually smaller. In Inverness, if a word can be shortened, it will be. 'Neeps and tatties', accompanied by a wee 'dram' (*see above*) and haggis is standard fare at a Burns Supper.

Ness Bridge: the River Ness, which arrives in Inverness nine miles after its journey begins in Loch Ness, has widened and become significantly shallower by the time it hits town. Indeed, one can almost paddle across it, pausing only to bypass the salmon fishermen in their huge wellies, although it's an impressive sight in full spate. Back in mediaeval times, it was considered to be the second-fastest river in Britain. I don't know what happened in the meanwhile, but sometimes it moves so slowly that it appears to be going backwards. However, its crossing has always been of strategic importance. In 1411 Donald, Lord of the Isles, on his way to the battle of Harlaw sacked the town and burnt down the old oak bridge, as he had fallen out with a local tavern owner, probably the boss of the Gellions (*see above*). A new wooden bridge was built but collapsed in 1654, and a stone bridge was erected in 1665, using stone from the Citadel (*see above),* supported by seven arches, A prison, containing two cells, was incorporated in the structure, which was swept away in a great flood in 1849. Eventually, after much argy-bargy, a splendid Suspension Bridge was built in 1855, with a big arch in the centre for traffic and coos, and two smaller side arches for pedestrians. The *Courier* printed a haunting refrain on this imposing addition to the local built environment, a fragment being 'In thee the past we bid adieu / And forward look to bridges new'. Does it not bring a lump to the throat? Progress then bade adieu to the grand old bridge, and the existing concrete span was opened in 1961, initiating the 'modernisation' of Bridge Street and its conversion into a deeply unsightly thoroughfare, described by Bill Bryson as 'awful, awful beyond words'. It is currently undergoing a 'flood works scheme': no doubt necessary, but marred by hideous stone cladding walls. In my youth, and even today, I refer to it as 'the new bridge', and I am not alone in this. Overshadowed by the Castle (*see above),* this little area must be one of the most unattractive spots in the long history of the town although, in fairness, Inverness has never laid claim to being the Venice of the

Highlands or, as Bryson remarks with serious understatement, 'is never going to win any beauty contests'.

Nights drawin' in: 'aye, the nights are fair drawin' in'. Inverness lies on a line of latitude which is further north than Moscow, so it can be a cold bugger of a place in the winter months. In the two or three months of what passes for 'summer', daylight exists until well after 10pm, although 'it's bilin' (boiling), the day' may refer to temperatures in the lower seventies Fahrenheit. Not so in winter. This phrase indicates that winter is on its way, a time of year when it starts getting dark not long after 3pm. Inverness is full of amateur climatologists but, as many are or were farmers, this is hardly surprising. (*See also* 'Snow on the Ben'.)

North Sea Oil: the discovery and subsequent exploitation of the massive Forties and other North Sea oil fields in the early 1970s created an unprecedented economic boom in the North of Scotland. Although a few large industrial employers, such as the Hydro Board at Foyers and the aluminium smelter at Invergordon, already existed in the Inverness area, no one had ever witnessed the sheer scale of the proposed oil-related developments. An economy based mainly around tourism, the public and service sector, agriculture, small business and light industry was transformed almost overnight into a major player in the international energy market and, naturally, US 'Big Oil' arrived quickly on the scene. Drilling for oil required oil platforms, and they had to be constructed near the oil fields on suitable littoral strips. In the Inverness area, Ardersier, a few miles to the east of the town, and Nigg, in Easter Ross, were selected as platform fabrication yards by, respectively, McDermott and Brown & Root, multinational, US-owned giant companies. Locals who had previously worked as farmers, labourers, shop assistants and so on were trained by the companies as pipe fitters and welders, something of a culture shock: one minute, an Inverness Council labourer; the next minute, Steve McQueen. There was traditionally a history of emigration from the Highlands, with young guys in particular desperate to get away from the place in search of employment. However, the new oil industry significantly slowed down this outward movement and even attracted emigres back to living in Inverness. The locals adapted well to their new roles, and the Inverness economy thrived on the wages which many of these McDermott guys spent in the town. House prices in the area soared, and at times there was almost a Wild West feel about the place. The Americans, mainly from Louisiana and the US Gulf Coast, fitted in cordially with the locals, and were friendly people, although they had problems with our accent: for instance, a contributor to this book had his surname changed from Urquhart, a name they couldn't handle, to Haycart. Also, a sizeable contingent of skilled workers, usually welders, arrived from the north of England, but they were frequently patronising towards the local employees, as indicated by the following lines which one of them had scribbled on a toilet wall: 'McDermott's men came down the glen / They looked like ballet dancers / One in nine had served their time / The rest were bloody chancers'. But the local employees were industrious, capable workers, even when they had to work at heights of up to 400 feet in baskets supported by cranes. Indeed, guys known as 'steel monkeys' used to walk along girders at these heights, without any visible support, when they were constructing the deck assembly. It was scary just watching them. When asked by a journalist 'how many men work here?' a senior Yank replied 'about half of them'. However, this was meant as a jest (I think) rather than as a reflection of reality. Within Inverness there developed a culture of emulation and imitation of these loud-voiced, 'can do' Americans: the 'Plastic Yanks', so called because of their adoption of Redwing boots, Cromer caps, bandanas and denim. Being Invernessians, they were far from slavish to their new employers, but they were intrigued by the arrival of US culture, previously limited to their TV screens. The presence of the yard, and the economic impetus it provided to the region, allowed Inverness to develop a successful and thriving business infrastructure, which persists to this day. At its peak, the McDermott yard employed 4,500 people. Although it closed down almost fifteen years ago, plans have recently been approved to re-open the site for the fabrication of offshore wind turbines, providing over 2000 jobs. Many people, however, still remember with fondness the early days of the oil boom. It was fun while it lasted.

Nyaff (one syllable, with 'ya' pronounced as in the German 'ja'): although Invernessians are among the most charming, complimentary and easy-going people on the planet, they are also not slow to show displeasure when they feel that this is what a situation requires. Therefore, disparaging remarks are frequently employed, and this is one of them. The word 'nyaff' means a useless, annoying, hopeless and often deeply unpleasant person, almost always male. Although also in common parlance south of Daviot, 'nyaff' nevertheless ranks high on the severe insult scale in Inverness in terms of its withering contempt. The word was originally applied to irritating bairns, so it is normally linked with 'wee', but adults now also come within its pitiless compass. Typical contemporary examples include 'Yer aye gurneen, ye wee nyaff: shut yer gob', and 'why are ye buyin' a dram for thon wee nyaff?' Its origins are claimed by some to refer to the yapping of a wee dog (or 'dug'), but the words 'gnaf' and 'niaff', meaning something similar, are also found in several northern French dialects. ('Nyaff', incidentally, doesn't seem to have anything to do with 'naff', an English slang word which implies 'in questionable taste', but there is an overlap of meaning, so maybe a connection does exist.) But remember: if you're called a 'haddie' or a 'lammie' (*see above for both*) in

Inverness, then feel relief. These are minor rebukes, mild zephyrs of disapproval which will drift lazily over your head, if the alternative is to suffer the tempestuous drenching and profound indignity of being called a 'wee nyaff'.

'Och': a completely meaningless word, which precedes most utterances. Designed to give the speaker some time to think about what he or she is going to say. Its usage is ubiquitous and often comes before 'blethers' (*see above*). Frequently used in conjunction with 'mun' ('my dear fellow'), as in 'Och, mun, …' or 'aye' ('Och aye'). (*See 'Ach' above.*)

Onions: yes, a strange entry to find in a book of this nature, but Invernessians knew their onions. A Breton who lived in Inverness used to cycle to France and back every year to bring back enough onions, in his opinion, to feed the town (at least he said he went to France but he probably only went to Nairn (*see above*) to pick them up). Unsurprisingly, he was known as 'Onion Johnny'. Also, the same Breton family arrived in town every spring – complete with striped jerseys, berets, 'ooh-la-la' accents and bikes – to sell onions, which they draped over their bikes' handlebars. They stored the vegetables in a building in Brown Street in the Merkinch (*see above*), and went home when they had sold them. The paterfamilias had a winning way with local 'wifies' (*see below),* and he usually had a dram or two when he visited the houses. By the end of each day he found it a problem to mount his bike, which he then wobbled over the Black Bridge to his temporary chateau.

***Outwith*:** this is another unusual entry, you may be thinking: why mention a commonly used English word in an Inverness phrase book? Well, the fact is that 'outwith' is rarely, if ever, used outwith Scotland, as one discovers when living beyond the boundaries of Alba in 'English'-speaking territories. Inverness has long been home to a number of languages and dialects, one being Scots-English, which uses several English-derived words which are not used in England, eg 'outwith'. It is also changed by Microsoft's spell-checker to 'without'. The word is the opposite of 'within', and implies 'not part of' or 'beyond the reach of'. Remember the hymn 'There is a green hill far away / Without a city wall'? This, of course, should read 'outwith a city wall'. This is somewhat similar to the

Scots-English 'Where do you stay?' This confuses the English until you explain it means 'Where do you live?' (I remember once practising my German linguistic skills on a wee German kid and asking him 'where do you stay?' This, of course, came out as 'why do you live?' He burst into tears and his Dad nearly belted me.) Another example of assuming an English word is in common usage is 'messages' (*see above*). This little ramble is simply to point out that a word doesn't have to be Gaelic to confuse visitors to the Capital of the Hielands.

Ovine outrage: 'sheep shagging', or sexual intimacy with a sheep, who may be willing or otherwise. Calling someone a 'sheep shagger' does not imply that they are practitioners of such a heinous activity: rather, it is a patronising term of abuse applied to certain agricultural workers or country dwellers in the Inverness area, particularly if they are wearing outsize wellies. It is an insult which is a savage step up from 'cheuchter'. The act itself is rare but, as Mick Jagger reportedly discovered, not unknown. The pouty-lipped songster was about to buy a farm near Drumnadrochit (*see above*) and he asked a local, a 'whinner' (*see below*) known as MacLeod, to investigate the quality, physical and ethical, of local farm animals. Jagger was shocked the following morning to observe his employee in a compromising position with a sheep, and exclaimed 'Hey, MacLeod, get offa ma ewe'. He swiftly abandoned his plans to be a country gentleman and flew back to London on the next plane out of Dalcross. However, the lyrics for a song were germinating in his mind... (*See 'Unnatural practices' below.*)

Phoenix: One of the few traditional and genuine bars remaining in the town. Has always been one of Inverness's friendliest and most popular watering places. Its incarnation as a licensed Public House dates from at least 1846. Today Grade B listed and recently reborn as the Phoenix Ale House. Its five floors stand proudly at the junction of Rose Street and Academy Street. The splendid Oval bar is encircled at its base by an original glazed Terrazzo spittoon (handy), and contains an old beer pump powered by water pressure, although the equipment is otherwise thoroughly modern. The old function room contained a mural of Highland characters, many of whom probably drank there (and may still do). The clientele is varied, entertaining and often eccentric and used to include thirsty journalists and also workers from A1 Welders (*see Welders, A1 below*) in Rose Street. The

Proclaimers played a gig there a few years ago.
'I would walk five hundred miles'. Well, I flew
that distance from London to get there and it was
worth it. An oasis of welcoming civility and
grand beer as well as a nostalgic reminder of old
Inverness as it was.

Pibroch: (*pronounced 'peebroch', hard 'ch'*)
from the Gaelic word 'piobairechd', meaning
'the act of piping'. Also known as 'ceol mor'
('the great music'). The pibroch represents the
ultimate expression of the music of the Great
Highland Bagpipes. The tunes are generally
laments, salutes or played at gatherings, and
are normally long and elaborate. It is
essentially modal in form, with its
meandering, unstructured and complex
rhythms, changing time systems, grace notes
and ornamentation. The Gaelic word 'uriar'
(pronounced 'oorlar') means 'floor', and is
the tune around which a pibroch is based.
Pibroch music is haunting, eerie and quite
beautiful, reflecting the landscape and culture
of the Western Highlands. The legendary
McCrimmon family from Skye is identified
with the origins of the musical form in the late
16th century. To listeners trained in the
Western conventional style of scales and fixed
notes, pibroch music can be strange and

sometimes dissonant and atonal. However, listen closely and you will discover the true musical heritage of the Scottish Highlands.

Piece: this was what would have been known south of Daviot as a 'sandwich'. 'Workies' (labourers and skilled artisans) would carry a 'piece box', usually tin but increasingly plastic, containing, as its centre of attraction, a 'piece and jam', accompanied on Fridays by a Mars bar. The jam was normally bramble. This was consumed, along with a flask of tea, for 'dinner' (lunch) at one's workplace between 12.30pm and 1pm. The bread almost certainly came from Burnett's, the town's main bakery and a local institution. Burnett's opened in Inverness in 1922 in Academy Street and shortly afterwards created its own spacious, posh dining/function room on the first floor. Burnett's moved production to the Longman in 1935, and their deliveries were made from the 1950s onwards by then state-of-the-art electric vans (and not delivered by horse-drawn vehicles as has been suggested by a few whimsical romantics). The bakery gave rise to a phrase employed by local urchins: 'I'm that hungry I could eat a scabby horse between two Burnett's vans'. Burnett's was bought by British Bakeries in 1999 and then, alas, closed:

another slice (or scone) of Inverness history disappearing into the toaster of time.

Porterfield Prison: Inverness's answer to Wormwood Scrubs. Stern high walls surround this facility (the smallest penal establishment in Scotland, a temporary home to around 150 prisoners), situated, surprisingly enough, on the fringe of the Crown area (*see above*), and close to the now derelict Youth Hostel at the top of the Castle Hill. Described in the Scottish Prison website as catering to 'a large and diverse catchment area': 'catchment area', certainly. The town nick was originally based in the Castle (*see above*) and in 1902 moved to its current location, which was then in the rural parish of Porterfield. Between 1966 and 1972 it contained the controversial 'cages' – cells within cells – and these were closed after one of the most violent ever disturbances in a Scottish prison, when five officers and four prisoners were wounded. This unit re-opened in 1978 and was finally dismantled in 1994. The current Governor is the prison's first female officer of this exalted rank. She was appointed in 2013, her purple hair and ear stud (good on you, Gov!) not being seen as an obstacle to her promotion. You'll feel much happier tramping the shinin' heather than being stuck in this place, so please do not carelessly discard your empty Prince Charlie shortbread tin on the street. You never know who's watching. (*See also 'Law and order' above.*)

Postie: an elderly, often retired bodach (*see above*), with a peaked hat and a black uniform, who delivered letters. He was afforded respect and called Mr McDougall or Mr Roy. He arrived at 9am and was on occasion offered a cup of tea, and perhaps a scone. 'Och, no. I've a few wee parcels to hand out the morn'. Was never known to wear shorts.

Puggled: no traceable etymological roots, and so probably demotic in origin (however one meaning of the word 'pug' is 'wheat chaff', so there may be some connection). The phrase 'Ah'm fair puggled' means 'I'm dead beat' or 'tired out'. Similar to Cockney 'cream crackered' ('knackered'). Often heard from 'wifies' (*see below*) returning home with heavy bag of 'messages' (*see above*). 'Puggled' can be relieved by having a 'dram' (*see above*), but not too many or you'll be even more 'puggled' (but won't notice it so much).

Quaich *(from the Gaelic 'cuach' and pronounced 'kwaych', with a hard 'ch' as in 'loch')*: a handsomely impressive rounded bowl which is unique to the Highlands and which can be found across the Inverness area, normally as an ornament or commemorative trophy. Dating from early Celtic times, a 'quaich' is a shallow, two-handed vessel which traditionally is carved or turned from a single piece of wood and mounted in silver, although 'designer' quaichs, made from pewter or silver, discreetly adorn the stripped-pine walls of elegant drawing rooms in the Crown area *(see above)*. It is a favoured delivery device for whisky or brandy, either at metro-crofter dinner parties and posh weddings, where the bride and groom toast each other, or more formal occasions, such as 'kilty danny' Burns suppers and masonic 'hoolies', where it is often handed round for a general 'slurp' (who knows where these mouths have been: 'health fascists' would deplore such communality). A quaich is also often awarded as a highly desirable prize for winning golf, shinty or other competitions. Such contemporary prosaic preciosity stands in stark contrast to the practice adopted by the Gaelic Druids of yore, who used a quaich for delicately sipping the blood from the hearts of their sacrificial victims who, prior to their imminent demise, had, no doubt, been 'quaiching' in their boots.

'Right 'enuff': another Inverness classic, which indicates resigned acceptance of the veracity of a statement, combined with a petulant annoyance that one hadn't thought of it first. Can also be used in isolation: 'Aye, right 'enuff', Often followed by ', but…' to indicate a fact of which one's protagonist had not taken account. Occasionally employed with 'It's worse yer improveen' (*see above*).

'Right shower, a': a phrase also in common parlance south of Daviot, but its ubiquity in Inverness is sufficient grounds to include it herein. Refers to a collection or gathering of unprincipled, self-seeking crooks intent on making one's life a misery. Often precedes an even greater insult, eg 'och, they're a right shower of… thievin' whinners (*see below*)'.

Royal Academy: the Academy was always the middle-class, 'grammar school' in Inverness, teaching a wide variety of subjects to secondary pupils. It was founded in 1792 in (unsurprisingly) Academy Street, where it remained until 1895 when it moved to the

Crown (*see above*), its location until 1980. It was a state school, like most Scottish schools, with an enviable record of academic success. Run by a Rector, and with many teachers wearing gowns, to the untutored eye it appeared more of a private school along English lines. However, pupils came from all socio-economic backgrounds (including the West coast, whose female students had their own hostel on Culduthel Road, as some of us recall with fondness). The High School, founded in 1894 and incorporating the Raining's School, was, in the days of 11-plus, deemed a 'technical' school, its emphasis being on more practical subjects than the academic bias of the Academy. There was a fierce rivalry between the two institutions, the Academy being regarded as more 'snobbish' than the High, who sang 'Academy rats, take off your hats and bow to your High School masters'. This competition was particularly marked in football matches between the two schools. The Academy building in the Crown now belongs to the University of the Highlands and Islands, and the Academy moved to the Culduthel area in the late 1970s.

Sassenach: an occasionally derogatory, but not necessarily confrontational, word which today is most commonly directed at someone who is English. 'How wis yer English holiday, Jimuck? Och, it wisnae bad, apart from all them sassenachs'. Sassenachs, however, are treated with friendship and respect in Inverness. The only sassenachs who are routinely mocked are the English football team, but they deserve the abuse which is hurled at them. The word was originally a Gaelic term, ('sasunnach') for 'saxon' (from the Latin 'saxones'), and used to describe a person from the Scottish Lowlands. It then gradually mutated into a term used by a Lowlander to describe someone from England. It's the reverse of 'cheuchter' (*see above*): everyone northwest of you is a cheuchter, while everyone to your south is a sassenach. It's a sort of cultural 'pass the parcel'. But if you're holding the parcel when the music stops, what are you? A sasschter? A cheuchnach? As this entry is now becoming complicated, it's time to move on...

Scaffie: almost certainly derived from 'scavenger' and is the universal word for council dustmen, who make an appearance from time to time when the bars are shut. Also used as a reference to a particularly untidy individual's appearance: 'och, you look like a scaffie, mun'.

Scud, to go for a: from the Old Norse word meaning 'hasty', this is a common term south of Daviot, eg 'the clouds scudded across the sky'. However, in Inverness a 'scud' is an activity rather than a description ('I'm off for a scud wi' the bairns' or 'he was scudding all over the place'). A 'scud' refers to a journey of indeterminate length, frequently by car and normally on Sundays. It also meant mild physical punishment ('a scud on the lugs'), similar to, but with less physical force than, a 'lander' (*see above*).

Shinty: under no circumstances attempt to play this game unless you are a burly six foot four inch crofter, or your limbs will be at risk of serious damage. On the surface, similar to hockey and hurling, but much more ferocious than both. Predominantly a Highland activity, its origins are prehistoric and it arrived in the Highlands when the Gaels brought it over from Ireland. The main annual competition in the Inverness area is the Lovat Cup, between Beauly and the Fraser clan stronghold of Lovat in nearby Kiltarlity. Incidentally, 'Lovat' is Gaelic for 'a rotten, putrefying place' (tell that to a Fraser, and then stand well back).

Shipbuilding: from the 11th century onward shipbuilding, centred on the Harbour (obviously) and Merkinch (*see above*), was one of the town's main industries. For raw materials, oak was floated down the River Ness and fir came from Glenmoriston via the River Beauly. Records reveal that the flagship of the Venetian navy was built here in 1087, while in 1249 Hugh de Chastillon, Earl of St Paul and Bois and a prominent member of Inverness's Flemish community, accompanied Louis IX to the Crusades on a ship built in the Merkinch. In their mercifully brief stay here, Cromwell's men commissioned a frigate to sail up Loch Ness in search of Highlanders to subdue: a common pastime of invaders from south of Daviot. The ships then rarely weighed more than 50 tons. The shipyards were located on both sides of the river until the 1870s when metal began to supersede wood construction although the Thornbush Shipyard was building steel hulls until well into the late 20th century. One of their last major commissions was a 500-ton vessel constructed soon after WWII, although small, specialised boats are still being made here for purposes of marine recreation. The Merkinch and the Shore Street areas once abounded with sail-makers, rope-makers, blacksmiths and ships' carpenters, now all submerged under the recent tsunami of apartments and chintzy dwellings. (*See also 'Citadel'*.)

Shot: nothing to do with the grotesque Highland 'grouse season' when thousands of harmless birds are massacred by upper-class morons (read Burns' poem 'Song composed in August' – 'westling winds and slaught'ring guns' – to discover his views). Rather, 'gie's a shot' means 'it's my turn now'. A word normally used by bairns. Not getting what you may rightfully feel is your turn can lead to debate, argument and, finally, a messy 'boorach' (*see above*). 'It's no' fair. Ye've had yer shot'. An alternative local meaning for 'shot' is as a reference to the number of 'drams' (*see above*) consumed the previous evening: 'I had a good shot at the Crit the other nite, mun'. It is akin to 'blootered' (*see above*), but without the latter's implication of collapsing on the street. A 'shot' is more restrained, relatively speaking.

'Shows, the': an annual occurrence, when a funfair used to arrive at the Bught Park (*see above*). Main attractions included the whirling apparatus where young exhibitionist employees, fags in mouths, leapt insouciantly from car to car, their attitude being 'bet you wish you could do this'. Many temporary relationships of a sexual nature were formed at 'the shows' between the local youth, culminating in a speedy visit to the nearby Islands on the River Ness.

Silver darlings: otherwise known as 'herring': oily fish which swim in large swirling schools, the better to avoid capture. They have many predators, including dolphins and fishermen, both of which are prevalent in the Inner Moray Firth. Dolphins, incidentally, particularly the bottle-nosed variety, can be spotted larking and leaping about (unlike most fishermen) off Chanonry Point on the Black Isle, close to Fortrose golf club, where one of the fairways contains the last resting place of the Brahan Seer (*see above*) who literally met a sticky end in a barrel of boiling tar, possibly as punishment for missing an easy three-foot putt. A contributor to this book was brought up as a bairn in Ardersier, the name deriving from the Gaelic 'Aird nan saor' ('headland of the carpenter'), a spit of land a few miles east of Inverness jutting into the Firth across from the Point and close to the Hanoverian Fort George (*see 'Colonel Bogey' above*). His family home, which was then probably known as 'the rundown wee hut in need of a carpenter', has recently been refurbished and reborn as the Dolphin Bay Suites: from grotty to green tourism in one majestic, piscine leap. The Point is also the location of a lighthouse built in 1846 by Alan Stevenson, uncle of Scotland's finest and most perceptive writer, RL Stevenson. However, all this meandering is ignoring the point of this entry: the 'silver darlings'. The Kessock Herring was a common delicacy in Inverness, which from the 13th century was the main herring centre in the Firth. The fishing season lasted from October till March, the period in which these fish were growing into adulthood before flapping off to the Baltic. In the industry's heyday, driftnet boats landed barrels or 'crans' brimming with thousands of these small aquatic beasties every week at Inverness Harbour. Fisherwomen used to sell herring, for smoking or salting, from baskets around the town, and one of this book's contributors' grandfather sold them from a horse and cart. By the early 1950s the local canneries began to reject most herring as too small for commercial purposes, and catches were banned in the 1970s and 1980s so as to rebuild fish stocks. The trade died off in the

1980s, along with the herring. It was a romantic business, though. As the Ewan McColl song has it: 'I used to sleep, standing on my feet / And I'd dream about the shoals o' herring'.

'Skeean doo': although this term is used by Invernessians to describe a pigeon which goes to Aviemore for its winter holidays (well, that's what it sounds like), it is actually yet another clumsy English transliteration of a Gaelic word, in this instance 'sgian dubh', or 'skean dubh', which means a black dagger. Originally an antler-horned short blade, inserted in a leather sheath and used by a 'ghillie' (Gaelic for 'boy' or 'servant') to carve up dead animal carcasses, it is today an essential component of the Victorian-originated kilt and tartan parody of what constitutes 'Highland dress'. It is worn inside the top of the stocking, and it now has a purely decorative function similar to the sporran, laced pumps, silver buckles, frilly white shirt, Calum Kennedy (*see above*) bow tie and all the other paraphernalia worn to indicate that one is not a mere trainee quantity surveyor from Beauly (*see above*) but rather a ferocious, bloodthirsty Celtic warrior. A 'sgian dubh' is a stabbing weapon, and tradition has it that, once unsheathed, it must 'taste blood' before being replaced in its sheath. It is, therefore, advisable to avoid insulting a 'kilty danny' in a 'blootered' (*see above*) condition, as the weapon's decorative purpose may be temporarily forgotten by the outraged trainee quantity surveyor, with a visit to Raigmore Hospital being the inevitable outcome. 'Bidh faiceallach': be careful.

Skeenuck: a 'coast-wester' (*see above*), specifically from the 'Misty Island' ('Eilean a'cheo' in Gaelic) of Skye, notorious for its 'midgies' (*see above*), omnipresent rain and the fearsome 'Black' Cuillin Mountains, where many an inexperienced climber disappears, never to be seen again. Used to be reached from the mainland by the tiny Kyleakin Ferry, when it could be bothered to turn up and prise its passengers reluctantly from the stools of the quayside bar. The narrow strait was recently (controversially) bridged.

Snow on the Ben: 'aye, there's snow on the Ben' is a portent of the dark days of winter on their way. The 'Ben' is Ben Wyvis in Ross and Cromarty: a mountain easily visible from the town. The phrase is usually expressed with a gloomy acceptance of the forces of nature, although Inverness is not famous for its sun-kissed beaches, surfing, balmy breezes or palm trees. The observation 'but there's always snow somewhere on the Ben' does not diminish its totemic significance for the inhabitants of the town. The mountain's name derives from the Gaelic 'Beinn Uais', meaning 'Hill of Terror', giving further ammunition to local Calvinist weather forecasters. (*See 'Ben' above.*)

***Steaming in*:** The opening of the Inverness and Nairn Railway in 1855 was one of the most important events in the history of the Inverness area and the Highlands generally. The arrival of the railway network created new communities, boosted the fortunes of local agriculture, fishing and tourism and facilitated the development of organised sport, mainly football, in the Inverness area and beyond. In 1865, with its line now extended to Aberdeen, the company merged with the Inverness and Perth Railway to form a new company called Highland Railway. Inverness and London were now joined by several hundred miles of track, a few lonesome whistles blowin' and clouds of steam stretching from the country houses of southern England, through the desolate Gaelic beauty of the Grampians and terminating at Inverness station, just a shooting stick or two away from the 'hunting' lodges. Overnight, Inverness became a 'destination resort' for passengers, freight and the wealthy English upper classes heading for the grouse moors to slaughter a few million small birds. The impact of the railway, however, far transcended its capacity for touristic voyeurism. By 1921 Highland Railway employed around four thousand people and owned almost five hundred houses in the town, mainly built as an incentive to retain staff. Most of these still exist (the houses, not the people, although one never knows…) overlooking, from the northern extremities of the Crown area (*see above*), Station Square below, in the centre of the town. Inverness was the railway's hub: the Millburn marshalling yards and the Lochgorm engineering workshops provided apprenticeships and jobs for thousands of people over the years. It's hard to believe today that there were once busy railway stations in such towns as Fortrose, Ardersier, Dornoch and Fort Augustus, but these railway lines quickly became essential to regional communications and were at the heart of the trans-Highland network, whose tentacles had by1880 extended as far as Skye to the west and Wick to the north (as well as spreading the Yellow Broom whose seeds were carried along on the rolling stock to grow into the plants which can still be seen beside the decaying lines). On 1 January 1948 Highland Railways was nationalised and became part of British Railways, the hard work having been done. The book *Highland Railway: People and Places* is an excellent source of anecdotes on the pioneering days. One such concerns an event which took place during the erection of the Culloden viaduct, a majestic span of architectural wonder. The contractor, John Ross of Fearn, took a party of railway bosses on an excursion to the site, leaving Inverness at 9.15am and returning at 9.30pm. They travelled in a train of carriages, pulled by a traction engine at a terrifying 4mph: 'refreshments were served to the excursionists when a little over four miles had been covered, and it is needless to say that ample justice was given to the various beverages'. Nothing changes, then. Having reached the viaduct and inspected the works, they then 'prepared themselves for the principal item of the day – the luncheon' served by Mr Cesari of the Station Hotel. Later in the day, when all the food and drink had been consumed, the party made its way back to Inverness station and, after an exceptionally long stay at the Craggie Inn, 'the disembarkation at the Station Square was witnessed by a crowd which completely blocked the thoroughfare'. And then, no doubt, off went the dignitaries to the Phoenix (*see above*) to continue their fact-finding tour, having witnessed the beginnings of a revolution in transport in the Highlands.

Strive: of French origin and meaning 'quarreler' or 'contender', in Inverness this term described the actions of the father of a bride when he threw pennies to the guests from the bridal car. A strange word to use, though, before the onset of a lifetime of blissful harmony, but it was once common parlance in the Merkinch. Maybe it has a connection with the Cockney rhyming slang for a 'wife' – 'trouble and strife' – but this seems far-fetched.

'The now': meaning 'at this moment'. The phrase 'the noo' is often heard south of Daviot but rarely in Inverness. 'The noo' seems (to me, anyway) to be uttered in a self-conscious manner, and is somewhat of a parody along the lines of (but not quite as blatant as) 'braw bricht moonlit nicht' (Harry Lauder), 'hoots' (Lord Rockingham XI 1958 record) and 'help ma boab' (Oor Wullie). 'I'll do it the now' is the Inverness usage. Granted, 'the now' in Inverness can often mean the same as 'in a wee minute' or 'in a wee while', procrastination being an Invernessian hallmark. However, 'the noo'? Never.

Thrawn: used widely in Inverness and also south of Daviot but largely unknown in today's Saxon lands. Stems from Middle English, and means perverse, unpredictable, doggedly dogmatic, proud, cocky and fiercely individual. A difficult word to define with any precision. Many Scots are 'thrawn', best expressed in the phrase 'wha' daur meddle wi'me?' Invernessians are more 'thrawn' than most. Commonly used by younger people: 'why should I do what you want me to do?' One of the psychological motors behind Scottish innovation and exploration. Could also explain why the Romans were reluctant to move further north than the Scottish Lowlands. Historical records indicate that the Picts epitomised the virtues of 'thrawn'.

Thon: not a computer game, but a word which means 'that' or 'yonder', with reference to a place or person. 'Aye, thon centre-half is shite. They'd be better off with a lump of concrete': a common complaint when watching Caley Thistle (*see 'traitors' below*). 'Thon' can also be non-specific, ie 'thon's a long walk from Inverness to Beauly'. As ubiquitous as 'och' (*see above*).

Tinker: a term applied in medieval times to travelling craftsmen but which now applies more generally to 'travelling people' (who don't travel much), who retain their own distinct folk song and traditional story-telling culture. The local non-travelling community has adopted several 'tinker' words. The term 'tinker' applies uniquely, under law in Scotland and Ireland, to gypsies. Some travellers used to have an encampment at Stoneyfield on the A96 old Nairn road, just a mile or so east of the town on some land between the road and the Firth, but there is now a purpose-built space for the travellers close to the Inverness Caley Stadium. Many of the local clans have, in their time, been 'tinkers'. Also known, by uninformed and patronising observers, as 'whinners' (*see below*). Travellers tend to keep to themselves, and they make their living in their own mysterious ways.

Tomnahurich: a large hill to the southwest of the town, now the town's main cemetery. There is a myth that it derives from the Gaelic 'hill of the fairies': it actually means 'hill of the yew trees'. The Caledonian Canal (*see above*) trundles past its west side. Most Invernessians have a relative (or several) interred in its hilly acres. It's a pleasant environment for a stroll on a warm summer's day, which occurs every five years or so. The hill gives its name to a section of the main road leading westward out of the town centre. Apparently, a policeman new to the town was once called to make out a report on a horse which had dropped dead on Tomnahurich Street, and he had to enlist a gang of men to haul the horse back to Young Street because he couldn't spell Tomnahurich. An apocryphal tale, surely, given the high literacy standards of Inverness's finest (*see 'Law and order' above*).

Topping *(pronounced 'toppeen'):* not a reference to the final moments of Charles I or Mary, Queen of Scots (who 'had her heid chopped aff'), or even Walls' Walnut Whip. Nor has it much to do with 'sadistic sexual dominance' or 'a practice used to prevent seed distribution', as some dictionaries insist. Rather, it is a word used in Inverness to signify the ultimate in approbation and approval. 'I hear thon wis a grand bit o' dancin' up the Strath, Jimuck.' Aye, it wis toppeen, mun.' ('I enjoyed myself immensely, thank you.') This revelation of ineffable ecstasy is often, but not always, associated with being 'blootered' (*see above*).

Traitors: refers to the merger of Inverness Thistle and Inverness Caley to form Inverness Caledonian Thistle in 1994. Left Highland League after almost 100 years, and sold themselves to the Scottish League. Now in Scottish Premier League but have won nothing of consequence in their twenty-year existence. Considered a treacherous act by many. Clach (*see above*) proudly battle on in the Highland League, fulfilling their ancestral inheritance. (*However, a 'traitor' supporter has demanded a right of reply, as follows. 'The author views the past through rose-darkened glasses which is probably why we still love him. How many football mergers can you name in living memory? Read* Against All Odds, *by Charles Bannerman, which describes the rise of ICT to the summit* *of Scottish football, overcoming all manner of geographic, financial and bureaucratic barriers. Inverness Caledonian Thistle are now the biggest name in world football, surpassing Borussia Munchengladbach, which is only 23 letters.'*

Trauchled (*hard 'ch', pronounced 'trochled' or 'trachled'*): this word is almost so onomatopoeic as to require no definition. If you find it difficult to interpret it as meaning 'sheer, unbridled joy in the delights of life', then you'd be dead right. It comes from the verb 'trauchle': to exhaust, tire and struggle to little or to no avail. If you're 'trauchled', you're wiped out, physically and mentally, and feeling harassed beyond belief. Even the kilty frolics of 'The White Heather Club' (*see 'Hielan' dancing' above*) wouldn't cheer you up, although a few drams might help. Again similar to the Cockney 'cream-crackered': knackered. Originates (unsurprisingly) from the 16th-century Dutch, and trudged its miserable way through the Doric Lowlands to settle gloomily in Inverness. Never say 'cheer up' to someone who is clearly 'trauchled'. Best to leave well alone.

Uck: you may have noticed elsewhere in this small volume the frequency of words ending in 'uck': eg, nairnuck, skeenuck. 'Uck' is a suffix which is attached widely to Inverness words, particularly to names of people. Unlike its counterpart south of Daviot, which usually signifies distaste, 'uck' is used as a term of endearment and affection in Inverness. So, someone called William (or Billy) is known as 'Beeluck'. Likewise James (Jim) is referred to as 'Jimuck'. This is a universally male phenomenon. The Royal Academy once had a chemistry teacher whose name was Mr Thom, and he was known as 'Tomuck' (but not to his face). However, if a name is too short (Ian) or too long (Horatio), it's difficult to append 'uck'. It's similar to 'ie', as in Ronnie, Stevie etc. Please don't be offended by 'uck', should someone attach it to your Christian name. It doesn't mean that you make people feel ill (if you do make people feel ill, they have other means of telling you so).

Unnatural practices: specifically, indulging in sexual intimacy with animals. The deplorable vice of 'sheep shagging' is mentioned above (*see 'Ovine outrage'*). However, similar deviant behaviour with a creature of the equine persuasion is, for obvious reasons, even less common, except in Inverness. A local worthy of some notoriety in the town was once caught in *flagrante delicto* with a horse, which may or may not have been a willing participant. However, being unable to question the animal, the horse's owner summoned the police. The perpetrator's explanation that "I was jist takin' a wee piss and the animal backed inta me" was regarded as fanciful, and he was placed in a cell, pending enquiries. Feeling hungry after his exertions, he asked for some food. Ten minutes later, the custody sergeant opened the cell door, chucked in a bag of hay, and said: "If it's good enough for your girlfriend, it's good enough for you". One could say he was getting his just desserts.

Wee Free: a member of the Free Church of Scotland, which dissociated itself from the Presbyterian Church in mid-19th century (there is also a sub-sect known as the Wee Wee Frees, and possibly one now in the process of formation which will be known as the 'Wee, Wee, Wee Frees', but I digress). Wee Frees are evangelical and strict observers of the New Testament. Pilloried by some non-followers as dour, dark-suited, bowler-hatted and readers of the collected works of John

Knox (unexpurgated version). When in proximity to Wee Frees, do not dare move on a Sunday other than attend church with its two interminable services. They only permitted music in church in 2010, and that was a close vote. It has been alleged that, such is their tolerance and their pleasure in the enjoyment of others, a group of Wee Frees used to chain up swings in the local parks from early Sunday morning until late Sunday night in order that kids could involve themselves, without any frivolous temptations, in the infectious hilarity of the Sabbath. It has also been suggested that Wee Frees prohibited sex while standing up in case it led to dancing. Surely neither of these claims can possess any validity? However, Wee Frees were among the few groups of people who assisted everyone, regardless of religious affiliation or socio-economic status, affected by the devastating mid 19th century West Coast Potato Famine and its aftermath. They deserve our respect and admiration for having done this and, indeed, for much else besides.

***Weeker*:** an inhabitant of Wick, a Royal Burgh since 1589 and the main town and old herring port of Caithness, Scotland's northernmost county. Caithness is almost entirely flat, aside from a few bumps, and naturally treeless (aside from the unsightly and intrusive conifer plantations installed by the Forestry Commission in the mid-20th century), giving rise to the observation that 'Caithness has only one tree, and it's taken in every night to keep it warm'. However, it's an austere, windswept and dignified landscape. The county's name originates from 'Cait', one of the Pictish Seven Kingdoms, and it's known in Gaelic as 'Gallaibh', (the land of the non-Gaels), as the local dialect was Norn, related to Norse, until the 17th century when Scots English gradually took over. The Gaelic tongue is conspicuous by its relative absence (except in Thurso). Wick takes its name from the Norse 'vic', meaning 'bay' or 'fort', and the town's residents call themselves, and are known as 'dirty weekers'. This does not refer to their unwillingness to maintain a strict personal hygiene regime, but rather derives from the local word 'dirdie', meaning 'busy'. No flies on the 'weekers'.

Welders, AI: readers attracted to this entry in the expectation of discovering Inverness's role in machine cognition should look elsewhere, as AI in this context does not mean Artificial Intelligence. Rather, the letters stand for the surnames of two of the actors in this tale of

Inverness's once most successful and lauded industrial concern. In 1872, Cluny MacPherson, chief of the clan of That Ilk, established The Northern Agricultural Implement And Foundry Company Ltd (no fancy 'Next' or 'Apple' here: they did what the name said). Just over twenty years later, the local ironworks and foundries in Inverness were absorbed into the company, now known as The Rose Street Foundry And Engineering Company Ltd (or the snappy TRSFAECL for short). They then bought up a bankrupt Bradford welding business called Ashton and Ibbotson (yes, the 'A' and 'I'), changing their name again to AI Welders. Several of their welding processes were revolutionary in the world of ironworking and welding, and in 1936 their first major contract was for the manufacture of a number of automatic welding machines for Bren gun engines. They secured international recognition during WWII for the construction of PLUTO, seventy miles of 3-inch diameter piping to carry fuel under the English Channel from the Isle of Wight to Cherbourg, followed by the development of ultra-powerful welds for Allied fighters. In 1973, and after one hundred years of local control, they joined with a London-based company to take advantage of North Sea oil and its associated opportunities.

However, rapidly advancing technology and its associated economies of scale, combined with competition from the Far East, led to cessation of trading in 2013, another example of Invernessian innovation and skill falling victim to wider, external forces, and perhaps not helped by the Inverness tendency to play down one's achievements. They will continue to be remembered, however, if only for the 'hooter', reminiscent of an air raid warning siren, which reverberated around the town at 12.55pm every working day to mark the staff dinner break.

Whilies (*pronounced 'while-ees*): 'sometimes' or 'from time to time'. 'Thon leg o' yours still sore, Grannie?' 'Aye, whilies, but it's improveen'. Also, when used in the singular, ie 'whilie', it is normally preceded by 'wee'' and used to indicate a non-specific time duration. 'When are you gie'in me back thon tenner, Jimuck?' 'Och, gie me a wee whilie yet'. Or 'I'll be back in a wee whilie', which could mean two minutes or never. Procrastination is all in Inverness.

Whinner: derived from the prickly 'whin' or gorse bush, with which the Inverness area is infested (the 'cheuchter' (*see above*) equivalent of Japanese Knotweed, such is its rapid growth). The 'whin' was originally introduced to the Inverness area as winter food for cattle, the poor animals. A 'whinner' is a sly, devious and untrustworthy individual who would sell his grannie for a ticket to the Clach v Nairn County game. Not normally a freemason. Often linked with 'tinker', although tinkers have a proud history. 'Whinner' is the ultimate demeaning insult and, when employed unwisely, can provoke fierce 'boorachs' (*see above*).

Wifie: not necessarily, as may be implied, a married woman. A 'wifie' may be any female, although normally no longer in her winsome youth when she was probably known as a 'lassie'. The closest comparison is with 'cailleach' (*see above*), as both are connected to 'bodachs' (*see above*), although 'wifie' has more in common with 'mannie' (*see above*). 'Wifies' tend to be below 'cailleachs' in the socio-economic hierarchy. Often employed generically, eg 'whit d'ye expect: they're a' wifies', and as an irreverent term for complaining menfolk: 'och, he's just a whinin' wee wifie'. Importantly, you should remember that the increasing prevalence in Inverness, normally in bars and restaurants, of signs stating 'free wi-fi' refers to luring potential customers by the offer of no-cost internet access. It is emphatically *not* a misspelling of 'free wifies', and you would be most unwise to consider it as such, as a 'lander on the lug' (*see above*) is the least you can expect for such an egregious interpretation of the offer. Inverness 'wifies' are certainly not 'free': at least, I've never met one nor have I ever had the courage to ask. Such a befuddled misunderstanding is usually the preserve of those who are 'dottled' or 'blootered' (*see above*): you should lead these sad people to the Gellions (*see above*) and gently explain the horrifying fate they have narrowly avoided.

Winchin': a courting relationship, more formal than 'hockmagandie' (*see above'*) with a view to possible betrothal. 'Aye, they're winchin. There'll soon be bairns on the way''. Probably derives from 'wenching', defined in the *Oxford English Dictionary* as 'habitually associating with common women': nothing 'common' about Inverness women, though. The word may also be influenced by 'winch', ie pull in with a handle. This makes sense, as 'winchin' was often initiated by females, desirous of the respectability afforded by marriage. Highland men were (and are) rightly fearful of the consequences of disobeying Highland women, so marriage was indeed often the outcome of 'winchin'.

'Yer seein'it': yet another Inverness classic. It is a response to a request concerning one's mental or physical state of health and wellbeing. 'How y'doeen, boy'?' 'Och, yer seein' it, mun'. A more complicated answer than one may at first suppose, as the questioner then has to ascertain for him or herself what exactly he or she *is* 'seein'. Gives very little away, but this is normally due to the respondent's verbal laziness rather than any attempt at deviousness or intention to dissemble. Reminiscent of the quote (mis)attributed to Martin Luther when defining his Protestantism: 'Here I stand. I can do no other'.

Zoo: Inverness Zoological Gardens: frankly, for a day's sightseeing I'd give this a body swerve: not from any liberal, 'why should we fence in animals?' argument, but because it doesn't exist. This thrusting, dynamic city of almost 70,000 people doesn't even have a scrawny little public rabbit hutch where one can feed organic carrots to the fluffy wee creatures. If one could establish a zoo, however, the local wildlife alone would be a big attraction, though the beasties probably wouldn't much like it. Nevertheless, as an example of the candidates for inclusion, and chosen from the Inverness area, here is a tiny selection. *Mammals*: mountain hare, red squirrel, snow hare, badger, common porpoise, dolphin, grey seal, pine marten, otter, wild cat, sika deer, red deer, wild goat, lynx (in twenty years' time). *Coastal fish*: herring, dab, haddock, lemon sole, flounder, skate, grey gurnard, Yarrell's Blenny (!) *Invertebrates*: butterflies and moths (millions of them), insects (same thing, but no midgies). This is before you start looking at the birdlife, and some of the human population. And we haven't mentioned Nessie yet. Who needs lions and pandas when you've got all this? And where would be an appropriate location? I suggest the Highland Council debating chamber, which can easily generate enough hot air to keep our encaged fauna snug and warm during the chilliest of winters. If properly directed, any surplus hot air could probably raise the temperature across the entire Inverness area: just so long as it doesn't threaten to melt the snow on the Ben.